First Edition

STAR TREK REVEALED

THE SPIRITUAL DIMENSION OF THE ORIGINAL SERIES

Also by Carole Devine

Solar Arc Directions: How to Read Life's Roadmap
Exploring Astrology Correspondence Course (112 CDs)
Celestial Gardening

STAR TREK REVEALED

THE SPIRITUAL DIMENSION OF THE ORIGINAL SERIES

CAROLE DEVINE

SURLY BONDS BOOKS

2007

A
SURLY BONDS BOOKS
BOOK
PUBLISHED BY
BRUCE & BRUCE, INC.

"Oh I Have Slipped
The Surly Bonds of Earth...
Put Out My Hand
And Touched the Face of God"

John Gillespie Magee

Published and Distributed in the United States by
Bruce & Bruce Publishing
PO Box 64007 Virginia Beach, VA 23467-4007
www.devineadvantage.com

First Edition
ISBN 0-9721674-9-8

Manufactured in the United States of America

Cover design by Charles Randolph Bruce

This work is dedicated to my most excellent
and talented sons,
Joseph, Gregory, Ralph and Kenneth DeMott.

Table of Contents

Part One: Our Current Condition

Star Trek holds up a mirror showing us where we are on our evolutionary journey. These are our current challenges.

Part Two: The Struggle to Evolve

We are slowly awakening and choosing a higher way.

Part Three: A Vision of the Future

Star Trek prepared us for current spiritual and scientific breakthroughs.

Part Four: Astrology of Star Trek

There is a time for everything under the heavens.

Acknowledgements

An author is blessed when his or her creative efforts are supported and enhanced by friends and associates. I have many such people to thank.

My gratitude goes to Randolph and Carolyn Bruce for their patience, support, and willingness to take a chance on this book. To Bernie Morris and Peter MacKay for their meticulous editing. I thank Lucinda Smith who agreed with and encouraged the main concept and stood ready to assist at any time.

I am grateful to Bill Herbst, an authority on the astrological signatures of the Sixties, for all he has written that sparked inspiration for the manuscript. To my sister, Barbara Baney, who provided a quiet, stress-free environment. To special friends, Margaret Bensen, Sally George, Regina LoGiudice and Ann Tynes. Special thanks goes to Rochelle Hasnas for her suggestions that led to the eventual title.

Endless gratitude goes to Stuart Dean, not only for editing but especially for his research for the "Resources" section of this book.

Most of all I'm grateful to my three older sons, Joseph, Gregory and Ralph, who first brought my attention to *Star Trek* so many years ago, and to my youngest son, Kenneth, whose enthusiasm for *Star Wars* brought it back indirectly again.

And last, I'm grateful to the late Duane Urban who encouraged my writing and taught me so much.

Introduction

The television series *Star Trek* took us places in our imagination that most of us had simply never dreamed of, as omnipotent beings in other worlds who created illusion with a thought, and aliens who could bestow godlike powers on humans were brought to life before our eyes. The possibilities were immense as we anticipated next week's wonderful trek into the unknown.

Of course we always triumphed in every situation in the face of the seemingly supernatural abilities of aliens. We overwhelmed them with our less powerful mortal shortcomings, relying always upon our wits and moral fiber. Our Star Fleet officers discovered the inevitable Achilles heel and turned it to their advantage.

Who among us who were privileged to witness the original series when it first aired could forget the hushed sense of expectancy as we and our children settled down at the appointed time before our TV sets, the familiar theme music echoing around our living rooms, and the words "...where no man has gone before" ringing in our ears? There is no doubt that we were willing captives!

Star Trek has gripped the imagination of loyal fans for over four decades—a television phenomenon that leaves millions shaking their heads and wondering what the attraction is to a mere science fiction series that was initially believed to interest only children.

Many books have attempted to explain it, while other

sources have critiqued the show as if it required exposure for the nonsense they believed it was. Physicists delighted in tearing apart the "impossibility" of its science as though no progress or deeper understanding would have been made between the 1960s and those many years in the future. Meanwhile, there has been a constant stream of movies and sequels to satisfy the hunger of present-day fans. And the appetite for *Star Trek* continues unabated.

When *Star Trek* first aired, I loved it. I didn't watch it, but I looked forward to the night it was on because my three little boys would eagerly get ready for bed with no arguments and then pad into the family room in their pajamas and slippers to watch it before turning in for the night. It gave me a break.

I began to take more serious notice of *Star Trek* in 1986 when, at my husband's request, I taped reruns of the 79 episodes of the first series so he could watch them. While I was recovering from surgery in 1987, I watched them all again to pass the time. I then became aware of the metaphysical foresight and wisdom of Roddenberry's genius. I am not sure if he was consciously trying to influence mankind's evolution, but I have often wondered if some Higher Power had a hand in its creation, its spiritual message being so powerful.

Roddenberry developed the idea of *Star Trek* in 1960, and the first episode aired at 8:30 pm, eastern time, on Thursday, September 8, 1966. The first reaction to it was minimal. And it is difficult to imagine how coolly it was regarded, considering its universal legendary status today.

The *New York World Journal Tribune* fired a cynical broadside at the USS *Enterprise*, claiming the show did not belong in the science fiction genre at all. *TV Guide* lamented: "The sky's not the limit on this trek." And the September 14 issue of *Variety* doubted the show would stay the course, with the reviewer nonplussed that *Star Trek* had even managed to ascend to the heady levels of prime time television.

Despite derogatory media commentaries, the series endured for three seasons because of the passion of loyal fans who staged write-in campaigns to keep the show on the air. It had clearly touched a deep collective chord with mainstream America and brought a message for us that we wanted, or unconsciously needed, to hear. After all, with its microscopic budget, the studio sets were laughable. It had to have *something* of substance to hold our attention so cleverly that we overlooked the obviously cheap and unrealistic props.

The unique element about *Star Trek*, from its first showing, was its intelligence. So intelligent, in fact, that NBC rejected *The Cage*—the pilot for the series—in 1965, assuming it was too intellectual and highbrow for the average viewer.

A social statement found itself woven into the fabric of each episode. Some of these statements were obvious, like the one concerning the race of half-white and half-black people. Dramatic plots about controlling the free will of others were issues we could all relate to. It was as if Aesop, after two and a half thousand years of slumber, lived again. Above all, the idea that we live in an illusion and create our own destiny heralded what was to come in the spiritual development of humanity.

The idea of illusion versus reality was the theme of *The Cage*, which aired later as a two-part episode called *The Menagerie*. This theme was repeated throughout the series. And the social conditions of these future timescapes, where there was an absence of hunger and an enlightened attitude toward money prevailed, brought something positive to contemplate, rather than the gloomy end-of-the-world auguries that seemed then, and still, to dominate modern-day prophecies.

As we relished these adventures each week, we became conditioned to accept alternative ways of thinking about ourselves, about society, and the very future of our species. The notion of a species "evolving" and the idea of a "parallel universe" became part of our collective thinking. Who uttered such things in mainstream America prior to the mid-Sixties? In fact, when we read the works of Lynne McTaggart, Deepak Chopra, Wayne Dyer, Esther Hicks, Mike Dooley, Jane Roberts, and others who show how we make our own reality with thought and emotion, it does not seem so far-fetched, precisely because this series paved the way for our collective consciousness to admit that it might just be possible.

Another spiritual phenomenon was in its gestation during this same decade. Helen Schucman and William Thetford were in the process of scribing *A Course in Miracles*, which contained themes parallel to *Star Trek* but which would appeal to a different audience. Events tell us that when humanity has reached a certain point in its consciousness and spiritual evolution, facilitators like Gene Roddenberry and Helen Schucman appear to assist the birth of mind-challenging new concepts. Some of their ideas are included in this book to show this synchronicity.

3

Star Trek was far more than an entertaining show targeting children. It was and remains a profound, multi-layered statement introducing thought provoking ideas urging us to look at life, reality, and ourselves through a different lens. It is a legacy rich in metaphysical symbolism.

Past, Present, and Future

The episodes can be divided into three categories. The first are those that catalog our evolution up to the present day. These stories parade our sins before us. Some highlight ancient history's follies, some are allegories making a point that is obvious about our misguided attitudes, and some are clearly taken from 20th-century headlines. The show did not arrange the episodes in this order, but it is fascinating that almost any conceivable foible was covered somewhere during the series. If the series had done nothing more than this, we would have been well chastened from the Aesop-type moral that could be assumed from each story line.

The first section of this book begins by showing us Star Trek's vision of a truly evolved society, to set an ideal toward which we are all hopefully moving. Within this context, we then review some of the misguided attitudes presented in various episodes, because any book about the original series would be remiss to exclude them. They are so much a part of the spirit of the series. Whether writers intended to have some of their stories teach us on various levels of consciousness is not known, but this is precisely what happened.

The second section examines episodes in which the characters could make a higher choice—not fully enlightened, but certainly awakening. (Who are we to define "fully enlightened" when we are all still awakening?) Here are moral dilemmas where a fork in the road points to a higher or lower path. It wasn't easy to choose between some dramas because many of them have this theme, but some are more critical in terms of evolutionary credit or quantum leaps in evolution. This section is the bridge between what we have been and what we may become.

The last section is a vision of the future. What are we capable of becoming? It has been said that we use only a small fraction of our potential, and developments in the study of quantum mechanics suggest that mind and emotion are actually the root of everything. The two together mold our future, whether we try to control it or not. This law of physics will operate by default,

4

like a car on cruise control. This section revisits those episodes that display what we call "miracles," which we can try to achieve.

When *Star Trek* first aired, not many people had heard of or understood quantum mechanics, parallel universes, time travel and dematerialization of the body into pure energy. Later, many other writers and spiritual leaders built upon these ideas, and it is accepted that these uncommon abilities are now possible for the average person. It paints an attractive future in which we have some personal control over events instead of the events controlling us. It is a future where kindness and peace prevail and are the stronger forces. It is what we all hunger for. No wonder we love *Star Trek!*

PART ONE

Our Current Condition

CHAPTER ONE

Where We _Have_ Gone Before

Darkness cannot drive out darkness; only light can do that. Hate cannot drive out hate; only love can do that. Hate multiplies hate, violence multiplies violence, and toughness multiplies toughness in a descending spiral of destruction .... The chain reaction of evil—hate begetting hate, wars producing more wars—must be broken, or we shall be plunged into the dark abyss of annihilation.
~ Martin Luther King, Jr.

Anyone who has watched the original series of _Star Trek_ will remember the episode _Errand of Mercy_. Spock and Kirk arrive on a primitive planet to help people who are under attack by Klingons. We marveled that the old men comprising the council on their planet, Organia, were unconcerned about attacks by Klingons—or anyone else, for that matter. We, who are used to fighting back and defending ourselves, could not understand. After all, we are supposed to defend ourselves or at least stave off an expected attack by attacking first. It is only common sense. We also state that "freedom isn't free," meaning that we have to pay the price of battle and bloodshed or else someone will dominate us. But didn't you find something in yourself affirming _"Yes!"_ when the old men of the Organian Council were able to make the weapons so _burning hot_ with only their minds that no one could hold them and therefore could not fight? Didn't you wish _you_ could do that? Wasn't there something visceral deep down that just knew it was the way it should be? We always recognize the truth in our gut.

We then discovered how the old men didn't have bodies anymore. They had just "put bodies on," like garments, so their guests would be comfortable. They had evolved to a point of pure energy, which is what we are anyway. But they understood the principle and evolved, they admitted, to where they no longer required bodies. What a concept! No sickness, no cold or hot, no famine or death, no fat or thin. How liberating that would be. They were points of light. They were visible, but only as light. They communicated telepathically—and harbored no secrets.

This is the ultimate *Star Trek* drama that draws it all together. It is the vision of the future that may have been planned at our creation as our evolutionary intention. It seems impossible to us right now, but is it really impossible?

Over 40 years after the series' debut, we are getting closer and closer to the realization of such a reality. Many writers have explored the path of our spiritual development and potential. For instance, the idea of becoming pure spirit is explored in *The Celestine Prophecy* by James Redfield. Even fundamentalist Christians have approached this idea in their interpretation of the Rapture.

We are witnessing today how the power of the mind shapes the future. Many spiritual leaders are teaching through books, tapes and even movies (*What the Bleep Do We Know!?*, *The Secret*, etc.) that our personal futures are wholly dependent on what we are thinking and giving passionate attention to every day. Several books, such as *The Field* by Lynne McTaggart, explain this as the consequence of the laws of quantum mechanics. In other words, it is a law of physics on the subatomic level. The laws may be different from the Newtonian physics we are accustomed to, but they are immutable laws operating regardless of our opinions. When we understand how subatomic particles behave, and how their behavior can be changed simply by the presence of a human observer, we begin to understand the power of consciousness to shape our experience. You've probably heard of the Law of Attraction, which says that whatever you focus your attention and feeling on is bound to come into your experience. (The trick is to focus on what you want, rather than on what you don't want.) We normally respond to this law unconsciously, just as we respond to gravity without consciously thinking about it. The law of attracting what we think of most is perhaps one of the greatest spiritual, mental, and physical discoveries of our times. It literally could change the world overnight. Of the many examples of how it has worked in my own life, the following was the most graphic, albeit not the largest.

Back in the Seventies, I wanted an answering machine. I was a single mom with four sons, and there was little money left over for anything. Unity, the church I belonged to, taught that

8

if you make yourself a "wish board," it would attract what you put on it. It was a way of "reminding the mind" to pay attention on a frequent basis. I cut out a picture of an answering machine (chosen randomly—first photo I found) and put it on the board. I taught private classes in the evenings at that time, and shortly thereafter a man came to my office with a package under his arm. He wanted to exchange the package for classes, since he was a father of six and had little extra money himself. Of course, the package contained an answering machine. But, it wasn't just any answering machine. It was *exactly* the same one I had put on my board—the same brand and model. It was as if God was showing off or chuckling over it. Since that time I have had countless examples of this kind of experience.

The mind is all-powerful, like a magnet, and if we understand and harness its power, there is nothing we cannot do. We are told this in the Bible. (Matthew 17:20; 21:21; Mark 11:23 and many other verses.) Even though we profess to be a Christian country for the most part, it is amazing how we don't really believe some of the Bible's tenets. Therein lies the problem. We don't believe it. The belief in what we pray for has to be so strong that we know without a particle of doubt. Prayer, I've come to understand, is simply aligning one's mind and emotions with the objective of the prayer and knowing, before it manifests, that it must appear, because of the law of physics. This is why the Unity Church uses "affirmations" as a form of prayer. Affirming that something exists or happens is powerful in itself. It is an expression of faith. When we reach the point where we can affirm and *know* that the gun in an opponent's hand is getting so hot he cannot hold it, we will then know how to pray.

Star Trek, I am sure, was intended as pure entertainment, but when humanity is ready to evolve further, don't you think God would use whomever He wishes to be His prophet? You will see as we analyze these stories from the first series that they are so original and uplifting it would take a most inspired ("in spirit") mind—or group—to conceive of them all so quickly. It was developed as they went along, and in three short years a corpus of work was produced that was nothing short of breathless. It was abundantly creative. Basically, its overall message is the same as *A Course in Miracles* and the laws of quantum mechanics: we make our own reality, love is the greatest power there is, and we cannot trust that our senses are showing us anything but illusion.

9

The Beginning

Although the apparent objective of *Star Trek* was to take us places human eyes had never seen, when Gene Roddenberry presented his dramatic adventures, many of the themes he addressed actually came right out of 20th-century America.

The first series appeared in our living rooms during the brief span between September 8, 1966 and June 3, 1969. Each episode was written, for the most part, a week or two before it was filmed, with script alterations throughout its production. Therefore, it was probably difficult for the writers to ignore contemporaneous historical events.

The Sixties were volatile years in human history. It was a time of raging emotions, which spilled onto city streets through demonstrations against racial prejudice and the Vietnam War. Many of these demonstrations resulted in violence.

The worst racial riot in our history erupted in Detroit, Michigan, on July 23, 1967, with 43 people losing their lives. Prior to this, on July 12 in Newark, New Jersey, a riot left 26 people dead. Albert DeSalvo, the notorious Boston Strangler, was sentenced in 1967 to live out his life behind bars. And in 1968, before the third and last season of *Star Trek* was shown, Martin Luther King, Jr. and Robert F. Kennedy were assassinated.

This volatile period in our history produced a cornucopia of surreal events, and many of these scenarios found their way into the scripts. It resulted in a kind of documentary in *Star Trek* about the issues of the 20th century and, in fact, many centuries before then. There was abundant drama in real life to weave into the storylines. The writers required little imagination to think up plots, because there was a veritable storehouse of thought-provoking themes to be borrowed from the daily headlines.

When contrasted with other *Star Trek* episodes that did *not* focus on the depravity of society, highlighting instead our potential evolution into more enlightened beings, these episodes about our current condition provided a mirror against which we could reflect our state of enlightenment on our evolutionary sojourn. We could see where we were in our development—our journey.

10　　We could gaze into this mirror and recognize how far from the mark we were in our path toward saintliness as a collective species. So many of the dramas put historical events into a new context—like a Hitler-style of leadership flourishing on another planet, or the rules of the Mafia lived like some kind of twisted religion—that we realized it could all happen again. We recognized in this mirror that we were far from ideal in terms of how we treat our brothers, since so much in the episodes reflected the current news. Since this was entertainment, it was painless to watch but surely resonated at an unconscious level.

The core reasons for our unhappy human condition could be categorized into several types, but primarily we still seem to respond negatively to judgment and fear. These trigger something in us that causes a kind of temporary insanity. It takes an enlightened person to see that judgment and fear ignite defense in the ego, and when we get that angry adrenalin rush we fail to see matters objectively. We have difficulty detaching from what we may perceive as a threat. *Star Trek* addressed this many times and gave us clues about how to handle it or see it differently. That, by the way, is a mantra of *A Course in Miracles*—saying to ourselves, when we are presented with a provocation, "I can see this in a different way." Then when we are provoked to become upset, jealous, judgmental, or whatever, we can pause and reflect on why the situation is the way it is or what we can learn from it, or some other "different way" of thinking. This, alone, can heal your life.

Before we can grow in wisdom and assess the truth of a situation, we need to recognize what we are doing to *inhibit* it. It would also be wise to appreciate that every thought we have influences the collective. In subsequent *Star Trek* series we see an illustration of this in *The Borg*. It isn't a fantasy. We *are* all connected, which is why it is possible to be psychic. An *intuitive* is a person who is aware of this connection and can tap into it easily. When we think we can do nothing to influence world events, we are wrong. We, as a collective, can control the energies or vibrations we send out from our minds, which act as magnets drawing to us exactly what we think about and focus upon most. If you talk about fighting a war (against anyone at all) and become passionate about it—even in the name of patriotism and democracy—you will attract more war. It is a law of physics. It would be better to be passionate about promoting peace.

Judgment Causes Separation   11

Passing judgment on people before we know them is common in most societies, even "civilized" ones. What we often fail to understand is that when we pass judgment, we create a barrier that prevents us from getting to know people at all. It effectively separates us. This process leads to counter-judgment and defensiveness in the misunderstood person, and diverts us from our primary reason for being here, which is union with one another. We are here to return to our state of oneness, not to create further division.

A Course in Miracles addresses this theme head-on. It teaches that you cannot know your brother if you have already formed a judgment about that person in your mind. It contaminates further information about that person because the new information now has to go through the filter of the judgment, and we no longer perceive anything but the *image* we formed of the other person. *Star Trek* addresses this throughout many storylines, but the episodes where the theme is loudest and clearest are the following three.

The most apposite and virtually in-your-face episode is *Let That Be Your Last Battlefield*, which deals with racial prejudice. At least this appears to be the theme on the surface. Everyone "got it" regarding that human flaw. But the episode actually has a couple of sub-issues, as well. Most people, when talking about *Star Trek*, mention this one as their favorite episode in terms of containing a message about social mores. There are 79 episodes of the original *Star Trek*, and this one was number 70, appearing midway through the third season. Almost anyone you meet can tell you the story about the half white and half black men, it is so easily remembered. Suffice to say that Roddenberry was also effective in "coloring" the two main characters as being half insane with hatred, and "insanity" is actually a true description regarding that emotion. One, Bele, sees himself as superior because he is black on the right side, as opposed to his perceived inferior, Lokai, who is black on the left side.

This episode is not only about prejudice itself but is actually more about hatred and its ultimate result. It does not paint Lokai as a victim to be rescued or Bele as an authority to be respected. The *Enterprise* and the Federation refuse to get involved at all— and only promise them due process. They make it clear that they had risen above this insanity long ago because it was not logical.

We are introduced to Lokai first, when he is rescued from a shuttlecraft he has stolen for his escape. He has been running from Bele for 50,000 of our Earth years. This number is symbolic of the long history of this sort of behavior and its single-mindedness. It also can symbolically ask us the question, "How long are you going to practice this insanity?" The two have not been back to Cheron, their home planet, in all that time and have no idea what their countrymen are doing. They are focused on their hatred for each other and the chase.

Lokai stole a shuttlecraft, but when confronted he doesn't consider it "stolen" because he is a "victim" and feels he has a right to use whatever is available to free himself. We observe his *own* prejudice when he says, "You monotones are all alike—first condemn and then attack!"

Bele has an additional characteristic besides cold prejudicial hatred. He is also controlling, which often happens when one group or person feels superior to another. Not only does he arrogantly assert that Lokai is so inferior that he and "his kind" cannot be trained to rise above their station because of innate limitations, but he also condescendingly explains that his superior race has loved Lokai's people and shown unappreciated benevolence. Naturally, if one group keeps another uneducated and treats them as inferiors, the suppressed group will live up (or rather, down) to expectations. It is a form of control. Amazingly, this same controlling attitude is extended to include Captain Kirk. Bele actually takes control of the ship at one point using his mind. He demonstrates the ability to concentrate his thought and thereby control mechanical devices at will. He changes the course of the ship through his mind and considers it his right because he *can*.

This is a red flag. What if mankind developed such ability? Would such power require that we first develop the ability to restrain ourselves from expressing extreme negative emotion? Perhaps this is why a character like Spock is necessary to the series as an example of what one must become if we are to develop such ability. It is obvious when viewing this drama that putting that level of power into the hands of a seriously prejudiced and hate-filled, ultra-emotional person would be suicide.

Above all, the story demonstrates the futility of healing prejudice with hatred and fighting back. Returning the same hatred or violence only feeds the hatred, making it continue endlessly (more than the symbolic 50,000 years) or it utterly destroys, as demonstrated when Bele and Lokai arrive on their own planet and find it has destroyed itself through its relentless hatred and violence. There is little left but huge numbers of unburied corpses. Even so, they transport to the surface and blindly continue their insane chase—though there is now no one left to conduct Lokai's trial or to pass judgment on him,

13

except Bele.

We can be sure the millions of young people watching this episode never forgot its poignant lesson. Whenever there is a hero like Captain Kirk, with more than two years behind him of notable influence, his words must carry weight and impact the subconscious impressions we all absorb during childhood. It is possible that this dramatic presentation highlighting the insanity of superficial prejudice played a significant role in helping to heal the tensions of America's race issue in later years as these children reached maturity.

Separation Breeds Ignorance

The Cloudminders, another episode from the third season, dealt with a similar theme. We witness a division, a clear demarcation line between privileged, educated, culturally elite beings profiting from the labor of a suffering lower class. In the same overstatement-of-the-obvious style, the upper class live high above the planet in a city built in the clouds, while the lower working class live on the almost uninhabitable surface while working far below in the mines on the planet Ardana.

The *Enterprise* visits Ardana to procure much-needed zienite, a rare element required to stop a plague on the planet Merak II. The people who excavate the element are called Troglytes and are forced to live in the harsh conditions on the planet's surface. They appear to be born naturally inferior, according to the leader of the cloud city's people, the Stratos-dwellers, and it is therefore considered that an education would be wasted on them. Some Troglytes are permitted to work as servants in Stratos. One of these is Vanna, who seems to be more intelligent than other Troglytes. She is heading a resistance movement against the harsh conditions under which the Troglytes live and refuses to supply the *Enterprise* with the precious zienite they need. Indeed, the Disrupters, as her followers are called, have ceased mining altogether.

As we saw in *Let That Be Your Last Battlefield* concerning racial prejudice, in which the prevalent theory is that the downtrodden race are not trainable or able to exist as equals in society with those who are in a privileged position, the Troglytes are understood to be retarded and violent as a result of their origins. They are therefore fit only to work in the mines. The occupants of Stratos, the city in the clouds, engage mostly in artistic and musical pursuits and cannot conceive what the Troglytes would even *do* if

14

they lived there. After all, they are not aware of logic or culture and could not possibly understand or appreciate such matters.

Eventually, Dr. McCoy shares information with Captain Kirk that zienite in its raw form emits a gas that renders those affected by it to appear retarded and behave violently, but the effects wear off with time. Kirk then concludes that the reason Vanna seems unaffected is because she was sent to Stratos to work as a servant and so was not exposed to the gas like the others. The *Enterprise* issues the Troglytes masks to protect them from the gas, and residents on Stratos are advised to change their attitude toward the Troglytes.

At first one might conclude that this story is about misjudging people when they are the way they are because of a chemical imbalance or illness. That is, of course, obvious and needs no commentary. And because of the equally clear symbolism of "those above and those below," it is easy to assume the central theme is about those who feel they are "above" others. But there is a more important issue: The division, that does not allow anyone on Stratos to be among the Troglytes (and vice versa except for servants) and experience their life condition, prevents an understanding of them. Since the Stratos-dwellers are the ones who make the decisions regarding the Troglytes' lives, it is unconscionable that they would do so without knowing them. It is also unconscionable that the people of Stratos gain all the profit from the Troglytes' work while the miners live in poverty. The question is, would they do it if they could trade places and live as the Troglytes live? They are not necessarily evil people—just insulated.

We call anyone who is not facing reality as "being in the clouds." Obviously, the location of Stratos was intentional to make this point. Droxine, the daughter of the High Advisor, Plasus, is a lovely young woman, seemingly innocent and pure. At one point Spock speculates that he doubts she would agree to the conditions under which the Troglytes lived if she knew about them first hand. She is literally "in the clouds" and far removed from unpleasantness and brutal realities, having been indoctrinated by her father to believe whatever she was told. And so the age-old theme of the sins of the father perpetuated through his progeny is also woven into the plot.

In the end, the need to experience the Troglytes' conditions becomes a necessity. Kirk closes off one of the mines, allowing the gas to be trapped and concentrated, and then has the High

15

Advisor beamed into it. Only when he is in danger of being contaminated himself does he relent and change conditions for the Troglytes.

A Canadian once told me that Americans are very insular and don't really understand the rest of the world at all—at least, the majority doesn't. That is quite true. We are for the most part used to our lifestyles and privileges; we can be most unhappy in other countries if we don't find these amenities provided. Values are twisted when we demand that our needs be met and do not adjust to where we are. It can be seen in the fact that very few Americans, compared to other cultures, know more than their own language. There is little effort to live among people in foreign countries just as the natives live. More emphasis is given to what a person wears or owns or their place in society than on the state of their spiritual understanding. I have even heard well-meaning people judge another person's *intelligence* by what they were wearing. This is of course a danger in all upper-class societies, but in the US it also trickles down to the middle and lower classes.

I met some Peace Corps volunteers on vacation in Costa Rica in 1995 who were so knowledgeable about how to fit into and enjoy other cultures, I found myself envious of them. I know a handful of people who have immersed themselves in a foreign culture and learned the language just to be more informed. From these encounters, it was obvious that their experiences had shaped them as more humane global citizens. Somehow they are different from the average American because of these pursuits. It is most likely that the majority of Americans would step in and *really* change some of the world's harshest conditions if they had to live in them for just a little while. We are not evil—just insulated.

Blind Hatred

Balance of Terror is another storyline in the prejudicial vein. One of the basic tenets of the series is that racial prejudice in this future time is a relic of the past. It is simply not acceptable in space travel. At this juncture in the series, Stardate 1709.1, the Romulans are an alien race, known only by their reputation; the occupants of the *Enterprise* know nothing about them—not even their physical appearance. However, it is discovered through secretly intercepted transmissions that they have pointed ears like Vulcans. A navigation officer on the *Enterprise*, Lt. Andrew

16

Stiles, has a deep-seated hatred toward the Romulans because of his own family's experience of fighting them many years before he was born. This hatred is a poisonous legacy.

The Romulans and Star Fleet have been at peace for 100 years because of honoring a neutral zone beyond which they do not enter each other's space. On this trip the *Enterprise* witnesses a cloaked Romulan ship enter Federation space and destroy four asteroid outposts, killing all inhabitants and pulverizing the asteroids.

Because Spock resembles them, Stiles transfers his hatred of Romulans to Spock. Later, Spock saves Stiles' life, but not before we see what obsessive hatred has done in Stiles' case, killing one crewman and effectively putting the entire ship and its crew in danger.

This debut of the Romulans introduces the concept of the cloaked ship, an entirely new obstacle for Captain Kirk's crew. A psychological battle ensues that is fought mainly with wits, since the *Enterprise* cannot see the cloaked Romulan ship unless it de-cloaks in order to fire weapons. Because the two captains are learning of each other as they fight the battle, they end up developing immense mutual respect. It is one of the more sorrowful scenes in the series when the Romulan commander tells Captain Kirk that, under different circumstances, they would have been great friends. This is a secondary plot about judgment and separation woven into the scenario. Once we suspend judgment long enough to really observe and know someone, it is quite likely we will see him differently. According to *A Course in Miracles*, anything that creates separation between us is the real cause of our lack of at-one-ment (atonement) with God.

We also witness a scene in which the Romulan commander reflects on his duties and expresses weariness over the constant killing and war. He says, "Must it always be so?"—realizing that war does not accomplish anything except more war. He hopes he will be destroyed before getting home to report that the enemy is weak and therefore giving his superiors provocation to wage war after so many years of peace. Having witnessed this, we find ourselves sympathizing with the enemy who, we discover, is much like us.

Incidentally, Sarek, Spock's father in later episodes, is played by Mark Lenard, the actor playing the Romulan commander in this drama. This was his debut on the series.

The cloaking of ships, so common in *Star Trek*, is something

17

we thought pure fantasy, but this year, 2007, cloaking is becoming a reality. The problem thus far is that the cloaked object's shadow is still visible. But that will undoubtedly be solved in time.

Fear of the Unknown

Any pioneer in space will encounter the unknown, the strange, and the downright bizarre. We, the audience, expect it and would be disappointed if such encounters did not happen. There are several episodes with this theme regarding an alien, whom we would initially fear, turning out to be, if not quite harmless, at least able to exist symbiotically with its surroundings and co-inhabitants after mutual understanding is established. One of the most poignant of these is the Horta in *The Devil in the Dark*.

It is Stardate 3196.1 when the *Enterprise* is called upon by pergium miners on Janus VI to locate and destroy an unknown creature killing their people. The creature's primary characteristic is that it can move quickly through solid rock and leave a tunnel behind.

This creature has killed more than 50 miners one by one in seconds by burning them to ashes with a highly corrosive secretion it uses to move through solid rock. The miners are naturally terrified of it since it is so fast they cannot fire a shot before they are burned to a crisp.

It would be expedient to kill the creature, as the miners request, but it has displayed intelligence by stealing a vital part of the system that controlled life-support functions in the mine. When they encounter it, Kirk wounds the creature, rendering it vulnerable, and then Spock mind-melds with it. He finds that she calls herself a Horta, and she is merely protecting her thousands of silicon eggs, which are being destroyed by the miners. She is the last of her kind and is responsible for these eggs to perpetuate the species.

The symbiosis here is clear, since miners tunnel through rock and this creature does it naturally. They conclude that after the eggs are hatched, the new Hortas can perform the grueling labor of mining, which would be natural movement to them, and the miners would be able to acquire their pergium and other precious metals with less effort. Thus, the two species acquire harmony.

18

The original series set the stage for decisions being made on the basis of information about the cultures from which the show's characters were drawn, rather than basing decisions on ignorance or assumption. The Vulcan mind-meld was a primary way of gaining information that couldn't be conveyed with words. In this instance, the Vulcan view about "infinite diversity in infinite combinations" gives Spock the trait of hesitating to destroy any life form before understanding it.

Naturally, if we encountered a creature like this, which kills instantly, we would be paralyzed with fear. Since mind-melds are not common, it is doubtful we would get a chance to find out why the creature would be killing. But here we are cautioned to wait—and to observe. Captain Kirk would have been dead in the blink of an eye if the creature wanted to kill him, but she was tired, wounded, and we find out later from the mind-meld, deeply sorrowful and suffering excruciating pain. She made no threatening move, so although Kirk could have destroyed the Horta, he resorted to the humane approach, which is to kill only in defense. Others may say he had a right to avenge the deaths of the dead miners, but if a creature is before you, wounded and not behaving as previously observed, it should at least arouse curiosity.

In this episode Spock tells Captain Kirk to kill the Horta when he gets the chance, but Captain Kirk is the one who hesitates, which is an interesting twist. (Previously, Spock had speculated that it may be the last of its kind, and it would be a crime against science to destroy it.) We observe Spock's stunning portrayal of the Horta's emotions, and learn how wrong they were to jump to conclusions about an unknown entity's true intentions. It may appear simplistic and obvious, but negative interpretation about what we don't understand continues to be the source of untold unhappiness, destroying countless relationships and costing thousands of lives. It is like a cancer we haven't yet learned to excise.

From the witch burnings in Salem to the current Muslim extremists' view that the United States is an evil empire, there is probably no society free from blind prejudice against something it does not understand—and what is worse, doesn't *want* to understand. To paraphrase *A Course in Miracles*, it is suggested that we forget all that we thought we knew about our brother, to be innocent of judgment, and only then can we "learn of him anew." 19

I once lived with a companion for a few years in a small town in Florida in the early Nineties. I thought at first I was getting along with everyone, since I received smiles and invitations, but halfway through my time there it all turned sour. I could not understand why I was so disliked, when I had done nothing to anyone and worked quietly alone on my business—which I did not impose on anyone. I didn't gossip and pretty much kept to myself except for social situations. I discovered after I left, through bits and pieces in conversation, about some of the assumptions people had been forming about me—with very little evidence. For one, I had left my car at my son's house in North Carolina because my companion's car was sufficient. At the time there was a heavy "traffic impact tax" on new cars coming into the state, and I saw it as a waste of money if later my companion and I didn't stay together long enough to be worth it. Someone concluded that I was too poor to own a car. Because I had a home business that was mostly mail order and therefore invisible (employees at the post office knew I had a business), others concluded that when I left Florida, I left because I couldn't get a job the whole time I was there. All this led many to assume I was living off my companion and not contributing anything financially, which was untrue. In fact, my companion managed all our money, which was combined. He decided what I would contribute and was very fair. I was astonished by all this erroneous judgment, and sad because friendships that looked promising and could have been fulfilling were not nurtured or given a chance. I believe this is what I regret more than anything else, since I consider friendship as my greatest wealth. The worst part is when something like this gets underway, it is almost impossible to influence people's impressions.

Another negative result, which I identified recently, is that I withdrew into myself after this episode and became suspicious and unfriendly in fresh encounters. I was guilty of assuming that whatever I said, no matter how innocently, would be used against me and people would have fuel for negative impressions. I was hostile and bitter for about ten years before realizing the poison had infected me, too.

Everything begins on a personal level in one-on-one situations and extends to the collective level. The more this kind of judgment-passing goes on in personal daily life, the more the group will express it on a national level. After all, the collective group is just a projection of the individuals—from the family to the nation. If we want to change the way our country does things, it will not work to protest or "fight against" it. Rather, by

20

exhibiting what we would like to see happening—altering our own behavior to what it would be if things were more to our liking—then real change can be effected. We could start by loving others unconditionally, and rather than pass judgment by what we *think* is true, treat others with understanding and compassion. Gandhi was a master at this and responsible for effecting change in his country. Mother Teresa declared she would never attend a protest or anti-war rally, but if one invited her to a rally for promoting peace, she would attend. If you are against war, you are adding energy to war. It is better to rally *for* a positive thing than to fight against what you do not want. To fight against anything is to be warlike. And being warlike gives energy to war in general and promotes more of the same.

Inner and Outer Realities

Perception is everything. *A Course in Miracles* teaches that perception is dependent on what we see inside ourselves, which *interprets* outer reality. It is a form of projection. The weaker we see ourselves, the more we have a need to exaggerate our persona to compensate. Likewise, the weaker we perceive ourselves, the more likely we are to give our power away. *The Corbomite Maneuver* is another dramatic presentation concerning fear of the unknown. Even more, it is an example of this illusion of power exaggerated proportionately with the self-perceived inner weakness of the one projecting.

The *Enterprise* encounters a buoy in an uncharted part of space. It is apparently a warning buoy, but since it is radioactive the *Enterprise* destroys it. Afterward, a massive spaceship called the *Fesarius* traps the *Enterprise* in a tractor beam, and a voice threatens to destroy them, giving them ten minutes to "prepare with their deity" before they die. The voice and face of *Fesarius'* commander, Balok, are frightening and authoritarian.

This alien presents itself as powerful, since its ship is at least a mile in diameter. Like an aggressive bully, Commander Balok will not listen to anything Captain Kirk says—or abandon his threat to destroy the *Enterprise* for no logical reason. The navigator, Lieutenant Dave Bailey, is so frightened he displays near hysteria, believing he will die. Captain Kirk wisely urges his crew not to panic—that the thing to fear is *themselves* and their reactions. His homily on fear sums up the whole point of this episode.

Spock, however, is intimidated, perceiving their position as weak, and is willing to admit "checkmate"—to give his power

21

away. But the reference to chess reminds Kirk of poker. Out of desperation, and in case the threat of imminent destruction is real, Captain Kirk bluffs and advises Commander Balok that under threat of attack, Federation ships have a self-destruct system called "corbomite," which will simultaneously kill the attacker. This averts the imminent disaster, since Balok is not sure it isn't true.

As the plot unfolds, we learn that Commander Balok is actually a small, childlike creature, appearing no more than two to five years old, who uses a puppet and an artificial voice for his on-screen persona, thereby appearing more terrifying than he is. Being unsure of the other's superiority, both must stand firm and put up a good front. It is another version of fear of the unknown, which leads us to do so much which is deceptive when inwardly we are uncertain.

This leads us back to the issue of premature judgment—our own assumptions (I won't be respected as I am, so I will assume a more terrifying persona) and judgment of other people's reactions, agendas, assumptions and so forth. Sometimes it can make fools of people.

Many years ago I was on a bowling team in a league from my workplace in St. Louis. I did not drive then and always needed to ride with someone else. I usually went with my roommate, who worked at the same place and was on the league team. One time I had asked and received a lift from someone I didn't know well and had appreciated it. Then one night it was uncertain whether my roommate was going, so I speculated out loud to someone that I supposed I *could* ask the lady who had given me a ride that one time before. But a short time later my roommate was able to go, so it was unnecessary to ask the other person. Later at the bowling alley, in front of everyone, the one I didn't need to ask for a ride confronted me in loud voice about "why I assumed that she would give me a ride. And didn't I think it would have been a good idea to *ask* first?" I tried to explain to her that I didn't need to ask because I didn't require the ride after all. Was I supposed to go to her and say, "I was going to ask you for a ride, but now I don't need one, so I'm not going to ask you, after all"? I would have looked stupid. But the woman was livid and wasn't listening or understanding. In fact, she was making a spectacle of herself. But in an effort to "look at this another way," as *A Course in Miracles* suggests, I have often wondered what was happening in her life to cause her to be so fragile that she would overreact

22

that way. There is always something behind erratic behavior.

Shape-Shifting

The Man Trap is not the finest example of how to treat unknown entities. Regardless of the way it ends, there is an element of understanding that we can take to heart as an example of how to do things better. Being only the sixth episode, the series was evolving, just as we are. Perhaps if it had appeared later it would have ended differently. This episode is another favorite, leaving us the indelible image of the "salt vampire."

The *Enterprise* has to make a stop at planet M-113 to replenish supplies and medically check Robert and Nancy Crater, who are archeologists, and as far as anyone knows, living alone on the planet. Dr. McCoy had known Nancy romantically years before.

We see her apparently "true" visage as approaching middle age with graying hair. It is obvious early in the show that everyone who looks at Nancy sees her appearance differently. In fact, she appears to each man as what each would consider attractive. Nancy Crater is actually dead, and in her place is an alien creature with the ability to assume any identity in the beholder's eyes. She lives on salt, and because she can extract it from a body at will, many *Star Trek* devotees christened her the "salt vampire." In an understanding with Robert Crater, the creature takes the place of his wife and he provides the salt. However, they are now critically low on salt, and the creature is ravenous. In a desperate attempt to satisfy its craving, the creature kills two crewmen by extracting all salt from their bodies. It assumes the shape of one of them and is able to board the *Enterprise* undetected.

This episode could be categorized as reality versus illusion, since the salt vampire is most skillful at creating illusion at will. Many of the episodes had multiple layers of metaphysical symbolism. It proves that the fans got the drift of the drama by the fact that they nicknamed the creature a "vampire." It was never called that in the show. Salt is as necessary as blood to a human being, so anything that can instantly drain the body of just one element is a vampire. Going beyond that, though, our life force can be drained by many people who seem like "energy vampires." It is widespread. Haven't you been around people who leave you wilted and drained of energy just from their presence? Even though it is unlikely that we would evolve—in our present physical form—to a place where we can duplicate the physical appearance of others at will, we do have an epidemic now of

23

identity theft. It amounts to the same thing and is as destructive.

After taking on identities of several members of the crew, including McCoy, the creature is eventually hunted down and killed. Professor Robert Crater, its defender, is also killed, and is the only one who had sympathy or understanding for it. Even though he had explained his sentiments, Spock encourages McCoy to kill it when he has the chance, but McCoy is reluctant, not because of its being the last of its kind, though; it was because he was not sure whether or not it was Nancy. He does, however, destroy the creature.

As I said, this was an early episode, aired while the series was embryonic and developing, and that may be why this reaction seems so uncharacteristic of the principals. After all, it is established later that Vulcans see infinite diversity in all life, and here we see a starkly different method of handling an alien killer compared to the way the Horta was treated. Even though it had killed over 50 miners, Spock said that to kill the Horta, possibly the last of its kind, would be a crime against science. It is discussed in this episode that the creature is definitely the last of its kind when Crater compared its extinction to that of the buffalo. And it had no eggs, as the Horta did, to perpetuate its species.

Robert Crater's explanation of the creature just trying to survive and being very intelligent could have swayed the *Enterprise* officers to stun and transport it back to the planet with a plentiful supply of salt to live out its natural life. Further, there was obviously no conscious effort to lend continuity to the show as episodes unfolded. It was seen only as science fiction entertainment. But Gene Roddenberry was a remarkable and compassionate man. His moral and social messages woven into the series show him to be something of a contemporary prophet. Who would have guessed in the mid-Sixties that identity theft would be the horrendous problem it is now or that there would be a massive shift in consciousness upon recognizing that we can create anything we think about?

However, there is another side to this—perception. We see what we want to see. Or rather what we are conditioned to see. Every second our subconscious minds take in millions of fragments of information, but we can only concentrate on or perceive a tiny fraction of them. What we choose as the "truth" of a situation is only subjective. In other words, "beauty is in the eye of the beholder," and the salt vampire was spectacularly aware of

24

this. She became what others wanted to see by extracting from their minds what they would consider attractive or important. Also, when we behold anything we think is attractive, we endow it with many qualities that are just not there. I once overheard a teenager say to a friend, "Well, she's so pretty, she *must* be sweet." (No wonder romantic love is so disappointing.)

If we choose spiritually to perceive everyone we encounter as an aspect of ourselves—and we are all one and therefore connected—how our perspective of each person's value would change! The concept of charity would change. *A Course in Miracles* says we give only to ourselves. After all, if we are all one, then I am the person I am giving to—the giver and the receiver. This is the concept behind the words, "Ask not for whom the bell tolls. It tolls for thee." Each person who dies takes a part of each of us with him.

CHAPTER TWO

Drugs, Placebos, and Disease

We are all wired into a survival trip now. No more of the speed that fueled the 60's. That was the fatal flaw in Tim Leary's trip. He crashed around America selling "consciousness expansion" without ever giving a thought to the grim meat-hook realities that were lying in wait for all the people who took him seriously... All those pathetically eager acid freaks who thought they could buy Peace and Understanding for three bucks a hit. But their loss and failure are ours too. What Leary took down with him was the central illusion of a whole lifestyle that he helped create... a generation of permanent cripples, failed seekers, who never understood the essential old-mystic fallacy of the Acid Culture: the desperate assumption that somebody... or at least some force—is tending the light at the end of the tunnel.
~ Hunter S. Thompson

Through television, radio and other media, we are constantly bombarded with a raft of issues relating to drugs and disease. Our senses are overwhelmed by ads about the protection of our children from drug experimentation, and conversely by ads that promote the use of drugs for just about any discomfort imaginable—from flatulence, bad breath, to "that bloated feeling."

The message is simple. If you are too lazy or too busy to maintain your physical and mental well-being, there is always a convenient pharmaceutical fix for sale. Children are quick to realize the underlying message that taking drugs brings a feeling of betterment. Consequently, we look in all the wrong places for that shortcut to our personal Nirvana.

However, our increasing knowledge and understanding of metaphysics reveal that many of our problems are rooted in the

26

mind. We believe what we are taught to believe, or what we *want* to believe. Why else is there always a placebo-taking or control group in pharmaceutical tests on drugs? Science has proven beyond doubt that some people will manifest all the effects of a drug if they are convinced they are taking it, even if they are taking only a sugar pill.

The Placebo Effect

Several episodes of *Star Trek* dealt with drugs—their effects on the physical body and on the mind. The Sixties was the decade when drug use skyrocketed, and it has been a huge global problem since. If one is cataloging the human condition of the 20th century, one cannot ignore this issue. One such drama, *Mudd's Women*, the fourth episode, appeared early in the series. This one is adept at displaying the power of the mind and our self-concepts.

It is Stardate 1329.1 when the *Enterprise* rescues Harry Mudd, alias Leo Walsh, a greedy and opportunistic individual. He is transporting a cargo of three beautiful women whose fate is to become the wives of lonely miners. His ship breaks up in an asteroid belt, and the *Enterprise*—at the cost of burning out three of its four dilithium crystals—follows them and beams the survivors aboard.

Although the transported women are not unusual beauties, they do appear to have a strange hypnotic effect on the crew. They are aware of this and exploit it. Actually, the unscrupulous Harry Mudd has supplied the women with the illegal "Venus" drug, which is reputed to exaggerate whatever assets are present in a person. It increases a woman's allure and feminine charm, creating an aura of irresistibility. It does the same for men, magnifying their manliness and masculine magnetism.

The women firmly believe they are entirely reliant on this drug for their bewitching appeal and glamour. So heavily do they depend on Mudd's exotic concoction, they find themselves panicking, filled with a sense of dread and urgency when it is almost time for the next dose. Eve, one of the transported women, expresses some misgivings for cheating, knowing in her heart she would be deceiving any future husband in the mines. But she still continues to take the drug to maintain her attractiveness.

Searching to locate new dilithium crystals, without which the *Enterprise* cannot function, the crew discovers a mining planet called Rigel 12, which can supply them. There just happen to

27

be three lonely miners on this planet, and Mudd contacts these men ahead of the ship's arrival to offer the women in exchange for his freedom. (He is being detained for illegal space travel.)

After the women marry the men on Rigel 12, the drug soon wears off due to a lengthy delay in the arrival of the next doses. The women's real appearances are then suddenly exposed to the men. Eve berates the miners for their superficial expectations, questioning what they really value about women (surely a lesson in itself). When it finally arrives, she takes the Venus drug in order to demonstrate the appearance of vanity, selfishness and uselessness. The metamorphosis is instantaneous.

It is only then that Kirk reveals that she did not actually take the Venus drug, but a placebo instead. He points out that she is alluring and beautiful, not because of the drug but because she *believed* the drug worked for her.

This is a crucial episode for the kind of society we had in the Sixties, because it demonstrates that we are what we believe ourselves to be, an idea just beginning to be accepted and embraced at that time. The women had a profoundly hypnotic effect upon the crew, which even the men themselves could not understand—not because they actually were more attractive than other women but because they truly believed they were, thanks to the Venus drug. Today, we are familiar with this idea, but it was not generally understood in the Sixties. Remember, motivational speakers were not so common back then. This was a fresh "aha!" *A Course in Miracles* repeats this theme constantly, but even that work was just being scribed in the Sixties and was not published until the mid-Seventies. Of course, we had heard of "inner beauty," but that was defined as good character, not as a self-concept.

In 1960 Maxwell Maltz published his innovative and classic book *Psycho-Cybernetics*. As a plastic surgeon he had noticed that improving faces did not improve or change lives as much as patients anticipated. He developed a theory that we must change our self-perception internally or our lives will not change no matter what we do to our external appearance. We now look upon his ideas as passé, since others have expanded upon this and discovered even more psychological insights, but it was a major revelation in its time.

In February 2001, I spent most of a day with a gentleman I had never met before, had no personal involvement with, and haven't seen since, so my observations were totally detached. We had two meals in different restaurants that day and, in retrospect, I consider the time a gift because of the unusual phenomenon I observed. There was nothing physically special about the man. He was in his seventies and not in the greatest shape. He was dressed casually. He did not say or do anything extraordinary. The two waitresses we had were in different restaurants and did not seem alike in any way. Yet, both of them treated him exactly the same way—and this treatment *was* extraordinary. They were outrageously playful with him, making jokes and engaging in clever and amusing banter. This to an extent I had never seen before or since. He had done nothing at all to initiate it and did not respond in a way that was out of the ordinary, although he was sufficiently humorous not to discourage the ladies. The first time, I just thought it was the personality of the waitress, but the second time I looked around to see if the second waitress treated others at the adjoining tables the same way. She didn't.

I was amazed, since I'd never witnessed two examples of this behavior back-to-back and so had not realized how graphically it can be demonstrated that we *unconsciously invite* specific treatment from people without saying a word. Now, in reviewing the conversation with him, I remember he mentioned that he liked people who had the gift of humorous repartee. He related stories of innovative things he had accomplished. The people he admired most were those with wonderful mental acuity. It was obvious from some of his accomplishments that he saw himself as articulate and quick witted. He was transmitting a subliminal message that he would appreciate a clever turn of phrase, and both waitresses responded unconsciously as if right on cue.

In short, we are what we *think* we are, and that is what other people will perceive and believe as well. We transmit messages from our subconscious to other people's subconscious. There are actually two conversations going on whenever we encounter another person. One is conscious—the words we vocalize and our body language. The other is subliminal—subconscious to subconscious. Robert Monroe explains this in his book, *Journeys Out of the Body*. This is the mechanism behind which people keep attracting the same experiences and types of people into their lives repeatedly. A battered woman will attract others who will batter her until she changes her expectations on a deep subconscious level. We are like radio stations transmitting signals all the time.

Mr. Monroe described his experience with an actual

29

conversation going on between his subconscious and another person's. At the same time, the other person was conversing with someone else and was completely unaware that the subliminal conversation was happening. What a revelation this is! Imagine that every time you meet someone your two subconscious minds are carrying on an entirely different conversation from the conscious one. That is how we get our uneasy feelings or completely trusting feelings about people we have just met. It comes from a very real phenomenon.

Further, we can deliberately influence the way others treat us by changing our expectations. In *A Course in Miracles* the fundamental revelation is that we are constantly "teaching" others who we are by our behavior towards them. Whatever we say and do, even unconsciously, teaches others what and who we believe we are. Confident behavior comes across in attitude and body language as well as words and appearance. If we are rude and obnoxious, we teach others how to be that way toward us. It demonstrates our own values and expectations. American writer and international speaker, Dr. Wayne Dyer, puts it this way, "You get treated in life the way you teach people to treat you."

Hypnosis demonstrates this. On television recently there was a street hypnotist who stopped people at random, hypnotized them with their permission, and suggested they were outrageous characters. They became those characters for as long as they were hypnotized but had no memory of it afterward. They were even told they were famous celebrities, and they believed it and acted the part. Thereby, we get a glimpse of what vast reservoirs of possibilities reside in the unconscious mind.

When we demonstrate our values and how we value ourselves, other people are sent a signal about how to respond to us. And if those we are teaching have not learned to suspend judgment, it is inevitable that we will receive the kind of treatment we request unconsciously. No drug can replace your inner self-concept.

Unnatural aging

Age. People lie about it probably more than anything else. Nobody wants to get old or to be perceived as enfeebled with age. Billions are spent on concoctions and surgeries to arrest the spread of proof that we are, indeed, getting "up there" in years.

Star Trek addresses the issue of age from two directions. One episode, *The Deadly Years*, trots out a tale of aging too quickly. Although drugs are involved in the cure, and radiation was the cause, the point is about experience versus age. It is predictable that the drama would conclude that experience counts. We know this on an intellectual level, and most cultures recognize it. The US seems to be out of step in this area. What we *say* about age is not what we *do*, as evidenced from hiring practices and the way we treat our aging citizens.

However, when drugs are deliberately created to delay the aging process—something we are seeing now in the 21st century—it is an entirely different story. It is enough of a battle reaching puberty without the Sword of Damocles hanging over your head, but this is the case with the principal character in the twelfth episode, *Miri*. The *Enterprise* responds to an automated distress call from a planet identical to Earth. Crew members beam down and discover a dilapidated city with a level of cultural development similar to our mid-20th century, although in a state of decay for about 300 years. They soon learn that all the adults are dead and the planet is inhabited only by children. With the onset of puberty, the children will die of a disease that affects only adults.

Miri is a young woman about to enter puberty and no longer feels connected to the younger children. Since she is also attracted to Captain Kirk, she tags along with the landing party and, at their request, shows them an old medical laboratory. There, among dusty notebooks, they find evidence of an ancient experiment to prolong life. The society succeeded in manipulating life spans to a ratio of one month equaling 100 years, which has worked, since the children are still so young after being alone for 300 years. They have only aged three months biologically. But a horrific side-effect of this drug is that the adults contract a disease that causes the rapid onset of madness, an ugly skin discoloration and, in short order, death itself. The adults had activated the automated distress signal to attract help before they died, knowing there would be no one left to care for the children.

Being adults, the landing party quickly contracts the disease, evinced by the tell-tale skin discoloration, so there is huge incentive to find an antidote. Working with the ship's computers, they are well on their way to discovering one, when the distrustful children steal the communicators and abduct Yeoman Rand.

31

One cannot help but compare this to Peter Pan, Wendy and the lost boys, although there are little girls here, too. There is even an older boy leader. Miri is an allegorical Wendy and, of course, the loyal children, yearning for parents, follow all their directions, including many rituals.

These children call themselves "onlies" because they were the only ones who survived the disease that took the adults. They distrust "grups" (grown-ups) because they had witnessed such violence when the adults of their culture had gone mad in the "before times" 300 years earlier. Therefore, they are adversarial toward the adult landing party, no matter how they are reassured. Ultimately, Dr. McCoy finds a cure for the disease, help is acquired to assist the children on their home planet, and the *Enterprise* moves on.

The first obvious point one might conclude about *Miri* is that we are always attempting to improve life through chemistry, only to create more problems along the way. It is a reminder of current drug ads in which an announcer with dulcet tones and a relaxing voice offers a product designed to alleviate a minor condition and then lists the accompanying side effects. A recent one even included the risk of lymphoma "in some cases!" When I first heard it, I thought I didn't correctly hear the words; it was so pleasant to the ear. When I heard it again, it was, indeed, suggested that lymphoma could be a side effect of this drug. The ailment the drug was purported to alleviate was nowhere near the seriousness of lymphoma.

Miri, however, speaks to us of more eloquent and urgent matters. Things like the abdication of adult responsibility, living by example, supervision, and structure. It speaks of the results of such abdication. These children, left alone without adults in their lives (albeit unintentionally), are longing for structure and rules. They even mention that one cannot play games without "rules." When conspiring to interfere with the grown-ups' plans, one little boy wants to volunteer to "get hurt" so someone will take care of him. When they hear of Yeoman Rand being concerned about the "little ones," the longing they feel is almost physical. In its absence, they resort to chanting and ritual as a means of fostering a sense of belonging to their group "family."

Most of all, they look up to a leader, an older boy, Jahn, to guide them and tell them what to do, and they listen respectfully to Miri, a substitute mother figure. Without any adult model to follow, except for older children, the place they inhabit is deteriorating and food is almost exhausted. They have no knowledge of maintaining themselves—the ultimate price of an unsupervised childhood.

However, adults do not have to die to leave children

abandoned. Symbolically, this episode sharply addresses *all* adult abandonment of children. It is most likely not an accident that the planet these children occupy is a duplicate of Earth, demonstrating what it can become if children are abandoned in many ways—whether through parents having no time for them, actual abandonment, or from too much permissiveness. Sometimes a parent can be "drugged" by the allure of other more personal pursuits that effectively remove them from the scene. All these changes in the family structure were a concern in the Sixties and have increased since then. *Star Trek* writers brilliantly integrated psychological implications of a society bereft of adult responsibility toward children in this one, and no parent could have failed to hear its message.

The Search for Paradise

The search for perfection and a desire for paradise are common, and we often try to find this particular Holy Grail through chemicals. Two episodes describe possible outcomes of finding Nirvana externally, which is an illusion in itself. In *This Side of Paradise* the chemical finds the people by spraying spores on them, and through the spores' effects, they believe they are in a Garden of Eden showered with eternal bliss. Many people remember this one because Spock falls in love and acts like a normal, smitten human being.

Predictably, in the end, they discover that it is non-productive, with no real satisfaction other than the moment-to-moment lack of concern for what happens next. But, Spock declares it's the happiest he's ever been. That was love, not perfection.

However, one episode in which the whole plot was crafted around a search for paradise was *The Way to Eden*. We are well aware of the vast number of diseases in our world, and there are many opinions about what causes them. The metaphysical perspective teaches us that the body heals itself, and so disease is unnatural; but if we deprive the body of what it needs for health, or if the mind is convinced that the body is not well, illness will surely follow. There is also evidence available that pollutants cause disease. However, in *The Way to Eden*, another cause is suggested.

It is Stardate 5832.3 and Captain Kirk spots a stolen ship, the *Aurora*, which he has been ordered to intercept. The *Aurora*'s resistance to a tractor beam causes it to overheat and explode, but the occupants are beamed aboard the *Enterprise* in time.

33

One of them, Irini Galliulin, is Chekhov's acquaintance from his Starfleet Academy days, where there was a romance between them. Another is the son of a Catullan ambassador, and because of this, Kirk is told to handle the "guests" gently and allow them freedom to roam the *Enterprise* at will.

The leader of the six-member group is Dr. Sevrin, who has a reputation as a brilliant engineer but who was dismissed from his post when he started moving back to nature and a primitive lifestyle. It becomes apparent that his reason is because he's a carrier of a disease called *sythococcus novae*. It is fatal to those not immunized, so he has to be isolated for the safety of the crew. Dr. Sevrin and Dr. McCoy realize this disease is recent and is caused by technology—artificial environments specifically. Dr. Sevrin is seeking an environment that will negate this disease but is unconcerned that he may infect and kill any life form he contacts. He has heard there is a planet called Eden and is determined to find it and settle there. Mr. Spock recognizes the man is insane, which is verified by computer records, but still promises to try and find this planet.

Irini, while visiting Chekov, who is assisting Spock in this search, discovers the ship can be run entirely by auxiliary control. This information is all Dr. Sevrin needs to commandeer the *Enterprise* and steer it to the planet that Spock has concluded is, in fact, Eden.

After stunning the crew and almost killing them with his ultrasonic rigging, Dr. Sevrin and his party steal a shuttlecraft and descend to the planet's surface.

When the captain regains consciousness, he and a landing party beam to the surface. Chekov is burned when he touches a plant. Examination shows all plant life to be poisonous and highly acidic to humans. One of the six followers of Dr. Sevrin is found dead with a fruit beside him, having been bitten into only once. The other five have taken refuge in the shuttlecraft after their bare feet were scorched by the highly acidic grass. Nothing is alive on the planet except plant life.

Dr. Sevrin protests at being taken aboard the *Enterprise* again, climbs a tree, plucks a fruit, and upon taking one bite, falls dead to the ground. Although the paradise of Eden looks breathtakingly beautiful, it is, nonetheless, lethal to them.

The Sixties brought us the "hippies," who were most concerned with getting back to nature, so it was appropriate to style Dr. Sevrin's group after them. They have the mannerisms, pseudo-costumes, hairstyles of the period—even tattoos of flowers and birds. Phrases, although modified, are reminiscent of this nostalgic period in our history. They are barefoot, have flowers in their hair, and even sit down in protest as soon as they are beamed aboard the ship. They speak of the "one," have a hand gesture to symbolize this, and respect no authority other than the one that resides within them. All of this was seen in the social mores of the time this episode was written and produced.

Perhaps Dr. Sevrin had a valid point, and perhaps *Star Trek*'s story was prophetic about this issue. As we advance technologically, our chemistry must change to some degree.

Being so accustomed to artificial environments, if air-conditioning fails we really *suffer*. And it is not simply our vanity. We are not used to adjusting ourselves to extremes of heat and cold anymore—at least in technologically advanced countries. It is also speculated that our health is affected by cell phones, computers, and emanations from television sets. To take it a step further, technology has brought us chemotherapy and radiation for treating cancer, each highly destructive to a healthy body. Knowing this, we can sympathize with Dr. Sevrin's viewpoint, but as he soon discovered, nature is relative to one's own personal environment.

Deliberate Biochemical Invasion

Chemicals alter consciousness, as we have discovered. The spores from the plants in *This Side of Paradise* were released in an impersonal manner. It is doubtful that the plants were fussy about which people they were infecting. Not so in an episode called *Elaan of Troyius*.

Elaan is the Dohlman of Elas, a planet that has been at war with Troyius for centuries. In an effort to effect peace, Elaan is offered as a bride to the leader of Troyius, and the *Enterprise* is chosen to transport her. An ambassador from Troyius, Lord Petri, comes along to teach Elaan the customs and manners of her new home, which she resists tooth and nail. It is plain to everyone how barbaric and primitive she is.

The women of Elas are said to be mysteriously irresistible to men, and Dr. McCoy reveals to Nurse Chapel that it is because an Elasian woman's tears have a biochemical effect that makes anyone who touches them that woman's slave—the ultimate love potion! Kirk is more than annoyed by the Dohlman's demands and temper tantrums, and when he threatens to spank her, she

35

changes tune and weeps that she is "not liked" by anyone. Kirk, not knowing about the tale of tears, touches them to wipe them away and console her, and is thereby enslaved by her charms. There is now no further talk of spanking. After this misfortune, McCoy becomes intent on trying to find an antidote for the tears.

Elaan, the Dohlman, is amazed that Kirk still takes her to Troyius and delivers her to her waiting groom. As McCoy finds the antidote and reveals that the tears create a type of "infection," Spock points out that the antidote is not needed because Kirk was "infected" by the *Enterprise,* his first love, long before the Dohlman.

The biochemical infection of Elaan is mild compared to the physical invasion of the amoeba-like creatures in the episode *Operation: Annihilate!* In this case, a portion of the invading entity is lodged in a body, which is controlled thereafter through intense pain. The entity's deposit becomes entangled with the victim's nervous system and even surgery cannot remove it. These creatures have been traveling from planet to planet, driving those they inhabit crazy with pain. By attaching to human bodies, they try to make the victims be their arms and legs and to do their bidding by inflicting unspeakable pain when there is non-compliance.

In both of these episodes, *Elaan of Troyius* and *Operation: Annihilate!,* people were controlled by chemical invasion without their permission. This is not the same as voluntarily giving someone control, as we explore in chapter three. This is a real intrusion. The plants in *This Side of Paradise* do not fit into this category, because they were not trying to control anyone—in fact, they were arbitrary about whom they sprayed with spores. But when one alters another's consciousness against his will for the purpose of control, it then becomes a despicable act. It is reminiscent of the movie *The Manchurian Candidate.*

We are reminded, too, of drugs to weaken the will of young women to make rape easier. This method is often used to gain control over lost or runaway children by giving them drugs that they do not realize will lead to addiction, and therefore dependency on pushers and pimps. These physical invasions could well be the most insidious crimes imaginable, wasting untold lives and creating profound personal misery.

CHAPTER THREE

Surrender of Power

In the general course of human nature, a power over a man's subsistence amounts to a power over his will.
~ Alexander Hamilton

There are two power themes in *Star Trek*. One is the danger of giving power away, and the other is misuse of power when someone has it. We can forget our own strength, creativity, and free will if we perceive another as being more in control or having a better way to do things. We all want to succeed in our endeavors, but if we doubt ourselves we sometimes look to others for guidance. An issue arises if we surrender our will entirely to one we see as wiser or stronger. And sometimes, without even knowing it, we become pawns for someone else's agenda.

Anyone who has ever watched this series for any length of time has heard of "the prime directive," which is a policy of Star Fleet not to interfere with any culture they encounter, no matter how much better (in their view) it could be. These episodes of the surrender of power involve this directive more than one might imagine. When one releases another from a controller, something has to replace it in some way. In replacing a lifestyle with another option, the releasing entity is imposing a view on the so-called "liberated" populace. It reminds me of our imposition of democracy on a nation we have rescued from a dictator. It is one thing to remove an oppressor but quite another to remake and impose an entire governmental regime without permission.

Further, if life is made easy, whereby we do not have to work for what we need, or if it has been done a certain way for a long

37

time with no power felt by the ones being controlled, people will lose incentive to think for themselves. One result is atrophy of the mind and the end of creativity. There are several episodes that address this.

The "WORD" Followed Blindly

In the series, some power issues arise because of documents that come to be regarded as law, as witnessed in *A Piece of the Action*. On the planet Iotia, visited a century earlier by the USS *Horizon*, the people are intelligent but highly imitative. The star ship *Horizon* had unintentionally left behind a book published in 1992, called *Chicago Mobs of the Twenties*, and somehow the Iotians have declared this *the* book on which their whole society is patterned.

The citizens talk like mobsters, carry weapons routinely, live with gang rivalries, and execute killings and "hits" daily. One gang leader, Bela Oxmyx, contacts the *Enterprise* by old-fashioned radio and requests a landing party visit him. He is looking to the *Enterprise* to supply him with weapons so he can take over the planet. Another boss, Jojo Krako, has the same idea.

Kirk believes it's his ship's responsibility to bring some sort of order to the planet since it was the carelessness of a previous Federation star ship that caused the breakdown of the society. However, he has to play by their rules, since that is what they understand. Therefore, he and Spock confiscate some mobster clothing and gain entrance to Krako's place with the aid of a boy who wants "a piece of the action" as his reward. For the one and only time in this series, Kirk drives a car He is trying to make a syndicate of the rivaling mobs, with the Federation receiving 40% off the top, but the gangsters demand proof that the Federation is stronger than they are. Krako is beamed to the ship so he can see their power, but later when all the bosses are gathered, the gang leaders still doubt the Federation's strength, since Krako only saw a few men in the transporter room while he was there.

At the time of this gathering, another gang is shooting it out in the street below. Kirk tells the *Enterprise* to stun everything in a one block area. That's good enough to gain the mobsters' awe and cooperation. When they leave, Oxmyx is the syndicate boss with Krako as his lieutenant. Kirk explains to Spock that the 40% will go into a fund to improve Iotia. However, Dr. McCoy inadvertently leaves his communicator behind, so who knows what they will find when someone returns?

The *Omega Glory* is another episode based on a culture arising from words in history used to define a culture. It also plays on the theme of identical parallel worlds, as we saw in *Miri*. In this one, the culture is based on a distortion of the Constitution, which is recited as their "worship" words, of which "freedom" is one. The warring factions are called "yangs" (Yankees), who are Caucasians, and Kohms (communists) who happen to resemble Asians.

Yet another fascinating episode that deals with ultra-controlling cultures arising from distortions of documents or philosophies adopted from a long-past era is *Patterns of Force*. On a mission to try and discover what happened to John Gill, a professor who taught history as "causes and motivations" instead of dates and events, the *Enterprise* is attacked by a thermonuclear projectile coming from the planet Ekos, which is not supposed to be so technically advanced.

Before going down to the planet to investigate, Kirk and Spock are equipped with transponders in their arms in case their communicators are confiscated or lost. On arrival, they immediately see soldiers, dressed (including swastikas on armbands) and behaving like Nazis, assaulting a young man who is a citizen of Zeon, a neighboring planet. Zeons could be equated with the Jews of Nazi Germany. There is even someone there called a Fuehrer in the shape of their professor, John Gill.

Although Kirk and Spock appropriate uniforms to be less conspicuous, they are exposed when Spock is asked to remove his helmet, thus showing his Vulcan ears. After interrogation about their weapons and communicators with no result even after a severe beating, they are locked up with the Zeon citizen they met earlier.

At this point, Spock uses the crystals in their transponders to rig a beam from a light bulb that unlocks the cell. They then go looking for their phasers and communicators with the help of their Zeon friend.

John Gill has apparently tried to help this planet (disobeying the prime directive) by modeling its government after the Nazis because he thought it was the most efficient system. He had not counted on recreating the evil part. His aid, Melakon, saw an opportunity early on for power, and keeping Gill as a drugged figurehead, Melakon is the real power behind the persecution of the Zeons. With the help of several Zeon spies in the Ekos government, Kirk, Spock, and now Dr. McCoy (whose help

39

was required to awaken the drugged Gill) infiltrate a meeting where Gill is making a rigged speech on television and calling for an attack on Zeon. Kirk and McCoy revive Gill sufficiently to help him denounce the government for what it has become, and putting the blame on Melakon. Melakon shoots Gill, and the Ekotians turn on Melakon, who also dies. Clearly the "prime directive" was violated here by Gill, with disastrous results.

Through this we relive the evil of persecuting an entire ethnic group. The Zeons were a peaceful people, not inclined to fight back. So, the Ekotians, once Melakon took over, felt confident it would be easy to subdue them. However, the Ekotians themselves were easily led as well. First, John Gill was able to organize their populace under Nazism because they were in a state of fragmentation and disorder when he arrived. He thought it was an efficient system if used properly. They were so accustomed to following the directions of Gill, the Fuehrer, that he was used as a figurehead by Melakon so there would be no questioning of his leadership. The people gave him their power.

At first glance, we laugh at how these people could give their allegiance and power to a "system" or a book that is old and whose origins are obscure. But this happens all the time. The Bible, for instance, is interpreted in so many ways that we have a plethora of religious sects based on various tenets. Each is certain theirs is the true interpretation. It was written in the original languages according to common usage at the time, and later, when the words had become obsolete and new meanings became attached to them, people inadvertently could misinterpret the original meaning. An innocuous example of this is found in I Corinthians 10:25, in which the word "shambles" is used in the King James Version of the Bible. That was the word for "meat market" or "butcher shop" in the time of King James in the 17th century. It is brought up to date and interpreted correctly in the Catholic New Jerusalem Bible, but how many Protestants are going to read that version? Fundamentalists adhere to the King James Version, but even the one they use is the fifth in a series of translations. The manuscript it was interpreted from had been copied many times over the centuries and might not be exactly like the original.

40

There were five translations after the initiation of King James' directive for a new translation—those being published in 1611, 1629, 1638, 1762 and 1769, the last being the one popularly used today. King James' lifespan was 1566-1625. The question is how many other words are not in use today quite the way they were back then? In fact, after all this time, how do we know that King James' translators got them right from a pure perspective without personal prejudice, or that the Bible, as we know it, is even intact?

In his book *Misquoting Jesus,* Bart Ehrman makes a case for the fact that the Bible's original manuscripts are not and have not been available for centuries, and since copies were done by hand—and in the beginning by amateurs—many changes and mistakes have been imbedded in the Scriptures. This book is something every Christian should read to get a more informed and accurate view of the Bible. It is not intended to downgrade or dismiss the Bible as unimportant. On the contrary, it is simply to alert us to the need for discrimination in what we allow to hamper our reason.

At the time of Justinian and Theodora during the Ecumenical Council of 553 AD, the works of Origen were decried, as were the writings of Theodore, Theodoret, and Ibas (referred to commonly as "the three chapters"). Justinian is known for his ecclesiastical tyranny. Before this council, reincarnation was an integral part of the Gospels. We see evidence of this in some scattered references, like John 9:2, when the disciples asked, "Master, who did sin, this man, or his parents, that he was *born* blind?" The key word here is "born." How can he sin *before he is born?* The answer that Jesus gave is irrelevant regarding this question of sinning before birth. The important thing is that the disciples assumed one can sin before being born and that one's congenital maladies can be a result of that sin. Jesus did not argue that point with the disciples. He answered as though it were a perfectly normal and valid question. Yet, if you were to ask a fundamentalist Christian about reincarnation, the idea would be scoffed at, although the majority of the world believes in it.

All this just demonstrates that even now many are infected with the blindness with which we give away our power and ability to think, discern, and deliberate our own truth. We just take someone else's word for what *they* believe is in our best interests, and some groups cause an enormous amount of damage in doing so.

I want to state at this point that I am very respectful of the Bible and am Christian in beliefs, but unfortunately, rather than bringing people together, the way the Bible has been used to further personal and group agendas, it has separated people more than ever.

41

Totally Controlled Cultures

Some episodes of *Star Trek* featured societies controlled by computers or long-held and unquestioned tradition, and in some instances, both.

In an episode called *The Apple*, the *Enterprise* visits Gamma Trianguli VI to check out strange readings a scout ship had noticed. It is Stardate 3715.0. A landing party finds the soil richly fertile and the planet-wide temperature 76 degrees. But all is not paradise here. Plants spray a substance that kills a crew member, and some rocks are like land mines. The ship's anti-matter pods are completely inert because of a beam coming from the planet. As a result, no one can be transported from the planet, and the ship is held in a strong tractor beam. Spock reads vibrations that are artificial in origin but doesn't know where they originate.

A storm erupts. Lightning kills one crew member and another, Ensign Mallory, steps on a rock "land mine" and is also killed. The party knows someone is watching them, so they flush out this person, who is so gentle that he cries when he is struck. He says he is Akuta, the eyes and ears of "Vaal," an invisible "something" that apparently takes care of these people. Akuta has antennae on his head with which to "hear" Vaal. The population abides in serenity and peace with no problems. They are immortal, hence no need for children, and they do not know the meaning of mating and reproducing. All they have to do to maintain this state is to feed Vaal, who somehow absorbs and uses the organic food they give him at intervals. They leave this offering of food in the mouth of an image that looks like a great serpent's head— symbolic, obviously, of the serpent in the Garden of Eden.

Now here's a dilemma. The ship is being drained of energy by "something" that they have determined is under the image of the serpent, and they cannot leave the planet. If they destroy what is under there, which will later be discovered to be a computer built in "the dim times," then they have interfered with the planet's culture.

We all have an innate need to be devoted to something, be it a political party, a sports team, our work, our family, and ultimately, God, but one would hope we'd have a choice. Even though this episode has been dismissed by some people as silly and a clear violation of the prime directive, we have to remember that the power of choice is at the heart of every aspect of this drama. The *Enterprise* can either release itself by destroying the computer (symbolically biting the "apple" in the Garden of Eden), or join

42

the populace on the planet and feed Vaal forever. The key here is that the "Feeders of Vaal," as they call themselves, did not choose the ways of their culture, either. They existed with it as long as they could remember and never questioned its existence or their role in it. Naturally, the *Enterprise* destroys the computer, and the Feeders of Vaal are freed to develop according to their own choices—including mating and having children.

Similar to this episode is *Spock's Brain*. This is one most people remember vividly. It points out that our brains atrophy without use. The inhabitants of this planet have the minds of children and do whatever "The Controller" wants. Why should they complain? They are well cared for, and when additional knowledge is required, they put on headgear called "The Teacher," which instructs them how to meet whatever crisis has arisen.

Another episode that features a computer programmed long ago and is now taking over to protect a society "for its own good" is *For the World Is Hollow and I Have Touched the Sky*. This one, however, is a spaceship disguised as an asteroid on a long journey. To keep the populace contented, it is controlled by a computer without their knowledge that this is a ship at all. They have been traveling for 10,000 years, but now the computer, called the Oracle, needs repair since, unknown to the inhabitants, it is on a collision course with a highly populated planet and does not appear to be correcting its navigation.

As with most of these stories about ultimate control, there is a pain mechanism to ensure obedience. If the wrong words are spoken, the computer hears and inflicts pain. It is the ultimate "big brother is watching you." The people might as well be puppets.

The Return of the Archons hammers home this point about mindless, automated control from the past in another version of this theme. This is also "for their own good," but the result is a zombie-like contentment and stagnation.

There seems to be a contradiction here when we compare this culture with the *Star Trek* culture, which also has removed the onus of having to obtain food and other necessities of life, leaving them free to pursue other goals, such as exploring the cosmos. The difference is in the total control over lives. *Star Trek*'s fictitious culture does not impose pain if one doesn't think or do things a certain way. Nor does it demand ritual or worship of anything, like "feeding Vaal."

43

Because This Is the Way It Has Always Been Done!

Most people follow what they have been taught—numbly and without question. Usually, if we see our parents go to church or vote, we do the same thing. We even copy their cruelty, if that is our childhood fate. The episode *A Taste of Armageddon* demonstrates the extremes to which this can lead.

In Stardate 3192.1 the *Enterprise* is heading to Star Cluster NGC321 to open diplomatic relations with civilizations there, carrying Ambassador Robert Fox with them for this purpose. Even though the planet they are approaching, Eminiar VII, is not responding to communications and there is a code 710, meaning that under no circumstances should anyone approach, the ambassador insists that they do.

When a landing party goes to the planet, they discover it has been at war with neighboring planet Vendikar for centuries. This war is carried out by computer, but to avoid destruction of property and disruption of societies, the computer decides what areas are hit and how many casualties there are. Designated casualties then report to disintegration machines to die. This is the way it has been done for hundreds of years and the people see no reason to change it.

The *Enterprise* is designated a casualty and the whole crew ordered to the disintegration machines within 24 hours. Kirk and Spock are imprisoned as hostages. If designated casualties do not die, the enemy knows about it, constituting a breach of the rules of war. The leader of this planet, Anan 7, is terrified of real war and fakes Kirk's voice to get the crew to the ground, but McCoy and Scott realize it's fake and they send no one. Kirk and Spock escape and destroy the disintegration machines and the computer. This forces either real war, with its attendant destruction, or peace talks. With the aid of Ambassador Fox, they choose the latter.

We depend on computers now to the extent that businesses would shut down without them, but what ultimate control they have when they decide who and when people should die! We are horrified by war, but the control here is so cold-blooded and deliberate it boggles the mind. It shows that when we get inured to the rigidity of custom, we are capable of anything. Are we headed in this direction?

44

False Gods

The Paradise Syndrome illustrates how we can bestow titles that are a bit lofty upon those who have superior knowledge. In this one, Kirk is knocked unconscious on a beautiful planet, much like Earth, and when he awakens he has amnesia. The people there, resembling American Indians, think he is some sort of god because of where they find him—emerging from an obelisk they hold sacred. Because Kirk knows some things they consider magical, he is made leader over their society.

The things he does are not magic. He, for instance, resuscitates a boy using common first aid. All anyone needs to do, apparently, is just know a little more than the average person and convince a group it is "magic." Often it is staged and the result of deception or propaganda. Gullible people will "believe" and follow like sheep. Sometimes it can be talent or success that dazzles us into believing someone is more special than others—or beauty. The list is endless. Witness the devotion of "groupies"—an amazing phenomenon.

Hitler, for instance, was a gifted orator who appealed to the needs of the lower and middle classes of Germany and improved their lives. Consequently, he was allowed to be a dictator. Of course it isn't as simple as that, but it is the crux of the matter. It culminated in World War II and the execution of six million Jews, which the German people would never have done had they been able to decide for themselves what policy they would follow regarding any ethnic group. When *Star Trek* aired, this atrocity had been discovered only a little over 20 years earlier—a blink of an eye in the larger scheme of things.

I spent six months in Germany in 1957 and saw many piles of rubble in Munich left from the war. When I mentioned something negative to a German woman about the atrocities of Hitler, she commented, in his defense, that they had "much better roads" because of his leadership. He was still being admired! None of this is ancient history—it is recent. Even now in the Middle East and Africa, ethnic "cleansing" is a daily reality for many terrified people because a few leaders are brainwashing thousands of followers. We are in need of awakening! ". . . for whom the bell tolls . . . "

Mind Control   45

There are other episodes in later chapters of this book that describe mind control, but there is a special one that belongs here with "surrender of power" because it deals with the process of gaining further control over major civilizations.

In the episode called *And the Children Shall Lead*, it is Stardate 5027.3 when the *Enterprise* answers a distress call from the planet Triacus. In a recent log recording of their group, one of the scientists assigned there declares that they have to destroy the "enemy within," and apparently he and the others have perished through suicide. Their children seem oblivious and uncaring about the adults' deaths. Spock believes an outside force induced the suicides but is stumped by the children's behavior. There is an absence of normal grieving.

After the children are taken on the ship, when they are alone, they summon what they call a "friendly angel" named Gorgan. The angel tells them what to do to control the *Enterprise*. The children cause all sorts of illusions (powers conferred by Gorgan), like Kirk's words becoming so unintelligible no one can understand him or follow orders. Others see things that are not there, which induces paralyzing fear.

A later reviewing of logs reveals that the scientists thought their minds were being controlled. They also discover that Triacus was once inhabited by marauders and legend has it that the "evil" is awaiting a catalyst to send it marauding again.

Spock and Kirk reason that an evil force needs a carrier, and Gorgan has chosen the children. They must either remove the evil or kill the children. Kirk plays back the recording of the chant the children used to summon the angel. The children hear it and gather as the angel appears. Gorgan tells them that Kirk and the others are gentle—a weakness—but while Gorgan looks on, Kirk plays video logs of the children playing with their parents when times were good, and then he suddenly cuts to the death scene. The children begin to cry, which releases Gorgan's hold over them. They watch as Gorgan's true ugliness is revealed. He then disappears.

Let's cut to the chase—if you want to completely control a country, train the children to be totally obedient and to believe you have *their* interests at heart. That is why Communist countries separated families and raised the children in camps.

Conversely, if you don't educate children at all, then, like the episode *Miri*, they will not be able to care for themselves as adults. Our country is in an educational crisis. Too many children are not finishing school, cannot read at their grade level, and are being left behind (despite Bush's "no child left behind" rhetoric). We are importing too much of our mind power.

I took some college classes in 2000 just to be more informed.

There had been a lot of advances since I went to school. For instance, the last time I had taken biology, genetics was not in the curriculum. To be fair, I learned a lot in the biology class. That one was good. But in another course, each time there was to be an exam, we were read the questions during the class before and even told on what page we'd find the answers. This was an average, well-respected college. I left the experience stunned at how low the standards had become since the early Sixties.

We may rationalize about spending tax money on war machines, but in the end it's the education of children that makes the real difference. Further, it's a downward spiral. If children are not well educated, then the teachers being produced are also not well informed. They cannot teach what they do not know themselves and probably do not realize how much they are lacking. One way for another culture to control us is to have to import those who are more educated to run our most important enterprises, and that will be the end of self-rule.

CHAPTER FOUR

Passion: Sensation, Guilt, Revenge, Jealousy, and Rage

It is a revenge the devil sometimes takes upon the virtuous,
that he entraps them by the force of the very passion they have
suppressed and think themselves superior to.
~ George Santayana

Ah, the juicy episodes in which we see human emotion spilling in all directions and causing havoc, disruption, and violence. What would humans be without it? *Star Trek* glamorized some emotions, making aliens envious. But human emotion and passion, when misdirected or unrestrained, can result in disastrous situations, and the series did not overlook this.

It is questionable that alien races would understand, much less want, our emotional experiences. Since we enjoy some of our lusts, *Star Trek* dived into the premise that others would too, but surmised that aliens would not be able to control them because of their novelty.

The Drug of Sensation

Catspaw, an episode involving aliens, is interesting from two perspectives, judgment and sensation. We do not find out until the end just what kind of aliens these are.

During Stardate 3018.2, Spock, Kirk, and McCoy beam down to the planet Pyris VII to find two missing crewmen and to determine what killed a third. The planet is dark and foggy, but the tricoder picks up life-form readings. The ship, however, does not register them. Suddenly they see a castle in the fog with its doors opening. A black cat is just inside the door. As they enter the castle, their life-forms cease registering on the ship.

Following the cat, they drop through a trap door in the floor and are rendered unconscious. When they come around, they are shackled in chains in what appears to be a dungeon. A door opens and Scott and Sulu, who were missing, enter in an obviously drugged trance, holding phasers on them and staring blankly. They use a key to release the shackles, and the three suddenly find themselves in a lavishly decorated room. A man called Korob is seated on a chair with the cat. He knows their names, and he has a wand in his hand, called a transmuter, which manifests a table laden with food. They refuse the food, so the man manifests a table laden with plates of jewels instead. Still they are not tempted, and Korob looks confused. He believed they valued these things.

The cat leaves, and soon a beautiful woman enters. Her name is Sylvia. The three seize the opportunity, grab Scott's weapon, and seem to have control, but Sylvia has a replica of the ship on a chain. She holds it over a candle flame, and on the actual ship the effect is blisteringly hot. They surrender, and Sylvia puts the replica into a block of what appears to be clear plastic, effectively preventing anyone from leaving or returning to the ship. They re-chain Kirk and Spock in the dungeon but keep Dr. McCoy with them.

Kirk and Spock notice that all the illusions the couple have created are manifestations of what humans would unconsciously consider either "scary," like the castle and the black cat, or "attractive," like the food, the jewels, or Sylvia. Therefore, the *Enterprise* officers surmise, these people are alien and unable to access their prisoners' conscious minds accurately for anything they can use with the intent to deceive. This gives them an insight about how to deal with the aliens.

McCoy returns in a trance with Scott and Sulu and releases Kirk to visit Sylvia alone. She explains to him that she comes from a world without sensation and the feelings of her assumed body excite her. She wants to know more about how things "feel." Kirk begins to romance her, while Korob watches from behind a screen. But Sylvia, like most women (possibly even aliens), wants to have affection returned sincerely, something difficult to feign. When she realizes that Kirk is not feeling the way she does, she has him removed.

49

Meanwhile, the ship has had time to weaken the force field of the block of plastic, and Korob releases Kirk and Spock, telling them that he can no longer control Sylvia or the other drugged crew members. Sylvia becomes a giant angry cat and crushes Korob under a door, at which time Kirk seizes the transmuter Korob was holding. He soon smashes the transmuter, and everything disappears, revealing Sylvia and Korob in their true alien form—very small, fragile, and insect-like, unable to survive in that planet's atmosphere.

A correlation we can draw from this is the way we assume things and form judgments with only partial information. Sylvia and Korob accessed the subconscious of the humans but did not have a complete picture. So their attempt at creating an intimidating environment for the *Enterprise* crew was a caricature. We do this everyday when we assume we "know" someone, when in actuality we just have a sketchy idea of the whole person. *A Course in Miracles* teaches that you cannot know your brother if you hold assumptions of any kind about him. These assumptions stand in the way, like a filter through which passes all new information, leaving you with a consistently distorted view of the truth. This has been mentioned before but cannot be stressed often enough. Most of our ills and spiritual destitution arise from judgment and non-forgiveness. It is astounding to hear a fundamentalist of any religion preach about brotherly love and, in virtually the same breath, approve of war and vengeance. The avatars and wise men throughout human history were not warriors. War, or killing in any form, was not on the plate of the spiritual food they brought us.

Then, of course, there is the obvious theme about sensation. Sylvia was lost in discovery of pleasure, like a drug, but this quickly turned to rage when she felt betrayed, all leading to her and her companion's demise.

Adjusting to human sensation and emotion seemed to be a major problem with alien species who took on human form in the series, and it was most apparent in the episode *By Any Other Name*. The aliens in their non-human form ended up being larger and different in appearance (which we are told about but never see), but the theme was the same. The officers of the *Enterprise* get one alien drunk intentionally, another angry, another lustful, and the fourth jealous. It was hilarious. However, as a mirror of our own behavior, it was a sobering episode.

In *The Conscience of the King*, we see how obsessive passion can lead to insanity. Twenty years before Stardate 2817.6, Kodos, the governor of Tarsus IV, had declared martial law because of famine and ordered half the population, 4,000 people, to a

50

painless death so that what he considered the more valuable half could live. He was supposed to have perished in a fire, but the body was never positively identified. Afterward, there were only nine people who had since seen Kodos alive (one of whom happens to be Captain Kirk) and knew or suspected he was not dead. Six of the nine are already dead— all murdered.

One of the surviving three, Dr. Thomas Leighton, a research scientist, lures his old friend Kirk to the planet by telling him he has discovered a synthetic food that will end all famine. It is a ruse, of course, and Kirk is annoyed that the real reason is that Leighton believes a Shakespearean actor, Anton Karidian, performing on his planet, is really Kodos "the Executioner," and he wants Kirk to verify it. The third surviving member is Lt. Kevin Riley, born on Tarsus IV and now serving on the *Enterprise.*

At first, Kirk brushes it off, but back on the ship he checks the data banks for the backgrounds of Kodos and Karidian. He finds that Karidian has no history prior to 20 years ago, and in comparing photographs, there is a strong resemblance. Therefore, he decides to attend a cocktail party to meet the company of actors. Karidian, he discovers, does not attend parties, but his daughter, Lenore Karidian, is there. Kirk flirts with her to gain information about Karidian, and they leave the party together for a walk. Along the way Kirk spots the body of Dr. Leighton, who has been murdered.

In order to investigate further, Kirk arranges for the transport of the actors to be cancelled so that he can perform that service for them, but he does it in such a way that Lenore thinks it is her idea.

Spock is curious about what he is witnessing and does his own investigation, which results in his deduction that Kirk's life is in extreme danger, since when the other seven of the nine witnesses were murdered, the Karidian Company was performing nearby. They put Riley in the engineering section of the ship, presumably to protect him without his knowledge, but he is poisoned anyway and after almost dying, recovers quickly.

Then a phaser on overload is discovered in a vent in Kirk's quarters just in time to prevent a massive explosion, which would have killed him and many others on the ship. Kirk then visits Karidian in his quarters and confronts him about being Kodos. Karidian reads a statement so that Kirk can compare his voiceprint with Kodos', which is on file. Later, when Kirk and Spock are looking at the voiceprints for comparison, Riley

51

overhears them and realizes that Kodos, who killed his parents, is on board. He steals a phaser and goes after Kodos, who is giving a complimentary performance for the crew, to kill him. Kirk follows Riley and prevents him from doing the deed.

Between acts, Kirk, in the shadows and out of sight, overhears Lenore tell her father that she only has to kill the last two who are dangerous to him, and then he will be safe. Her father is horrified, since he has lived with this guilt for so long and thought his daughter was the one pure thing he had in his life. When she realizes Kirk has overheard her, she tries to kill him with a phaser, but Kodos puts himself in front of Kirk, and she kills her own father instead. She is so insane after this, she believes her father is still alive and performing.

It is amazing how passion blinds us to right and wrong. We can justify anything if we feel strongly enough about it. This sort of thinking leads to war on a massive scale. It leads to attacks by fanatical terrorists who justify killing thousands for a religious ideal. It led to the Inquisition and who knows how many other atrocities. If we have a personal passion to protect or propagate, and we lose our objectivity, it doesn't take much for insanity to set in.

Identity Theft and Jealousy

Our identity is *not* our body. It is not our paper trail of financial data. Nor is it our job or our position in society. Our identity is our consciousness or essential spirit, our essence. Some might call it our soul. It is unique to each of us and impossible for another to assume. But attempts are made in our society today in worrying numbers to assume the lifestyle or status of those we deem better in some way. People in record numbers are confiscating others' financial assets, assuming false identities, or pretending to have credentials they have not earned, and because they are not authentic in aligning this fiction with their true consciousness, they are doing irreparable damage—not only to others, but to themselves as well. They will ultimately fail, and this is demonstrated graphically in the episode called *Turnabout Intruder*, number 79 and the last of the series. The basic emotion is passionate jealousy.

52

This episode also reminds us of possession of a body by a disembodied spirit, something I've witnessed myself. It is questionable where these disembodied spirits come from, but in deference to the Bible dictum, "By their fruits you will know them,"

I have suspended any judgment about some—particularly Esther Hicks and "Abraham," whose work is healing and positive.

I had an extraordinary experience a few years ago when a friend, a professional and highly educated woman, called me about her 13-year-old son. He had inadvertently taken a couple of incompatible drugs and lay for a few days in a coma. When he regained consciousness, he was her son in appearance, but another spirit had taken over his body. The new occupant told her who he was—a teenager who had died in an accident nearby. He was not ready to leave this life. Neither she nor her innocent son had ever heard of this kind of thing, so it wasn't her imagination. The last I heard, he was still occupying her son's body and had no intention of leaving. I *know* that this phenomenon happens.

In this *Star Trek* episode, however, the person is switching the spirits between two bodies. The woman, Dr. Janice Lester, commandeers Captain Kirk and puts her own consciousness in his body. Her intention is to kill the captain (now in her body) to have Kirk's body and position for herself, but she is unable to find an opportunity. The acting is glorious as Captain Kirk becomes rather feminine and the doctor rather masculine. She is jealous of his position, prestige, and power, which she believes she can never have in her own body. She thinks that by assuming Kirk's body, she will have his life. But the question "who are we?" is sorely tested here. Our consciousness betrays us. So much of our behavior stems from the unconscious and our lifelong conditioning that it is impossible for Dr. Lester to command the *Enterprise*, even though she had studied everything about it. Her temperamental outbursts and uncharacteristic decisions cause suspicion. Finally, Spock performs a mind meld to determine the truth.

Robert Monroe, in his book, *Journeys Out of the Body*, mentions several times that his consciousness went with him out of the body, and that his body was more or less forgotten while he was "gone." He saw with his spirit eyes, thought with his mind, which was out of the body with him, and essentially concluded that all that makes us conscious and that makes up our real identity is *not* in or part of the body. Our corporeal frame is apparently like a suit of clothes to wear while we are here.

53

A secondary theme is also included in this episode. During the mid-20th century, and even now to some extent, we were dealing with the inequity of males and females in career opportunities. We were just beginning to break away from the stereotyping of women in the traditional roles of homemakers, secretaries, nurses, and teachers at the time this drama was screened. Now, in the 21st century, women are catching up with men, and are occupying the more prestigious positions of doctors and lawyers, among many others. In this fictitious future time, none of these inequities exist, but Dr. Lester did not fail because she was a woman. It was because she was neither temperamentally suited nor trained to do the job of a Starfleet captain. Her unhappiness was caused by rejecting her reasonable options, not to mention her femininity, and becoming fanatically jealous of one she saw as more powerful and successful than she. It is an ego-driven form of insanity. In _A Course in Miracles_, we are advised not to be tempted to think we are treated unfairly. We alone are responsible for what we attract. Once blame is fixed outside oneself, trouble arrives on the horizon.

I have had experiences often in which I felt I was treated unfairly, but in retrospect, I can see where I caused my own treatment (we teach others how to treat us) and why it was necessary to have that experience to grow spiritually. That does not mean I handled it well—on the contrary. Just because we know philosophically how to live doesn't mean we always do the right thing. That is another reason to suspend judgment about people: one action is not a person's whole being. We all make mistakes and forgiveness is what is needed more than anything else in this world.

Revenge

Dr. Lester was sure it was being a woman that was the cause of her failures, but in _Court-Martial_, Lt. Commander Benjamin Finney is convinced it is Captain Kirk who is solely responsible for his lack of promotions. Years earlier, Captain Kirk had discovered an error in Finney's work and had logged it, as he was required to do, but Finney has imagined that this blight on his record is the _one_ reason he has not advanced as the rest of his class did. His rage and jealousy over Captain Kirk's success is fanatical.

On Stardate 2947.3 the _Enterprise_ encounters an ion storm. Finney, being the next on the duty roster, is told to go to the ion pod to take readings. Kirk follows procedures exactly and, pressing the red alert button, warns Finney to evacuate. After giving him time to do so, Kirk jettisons the pod. But Finney is still inside and is later reported dead.

They have to lay over at Starbase 12 for repairs from the

storm, and Kirk submits his report to the base's commander, Commodore Stone. However, the computer that generates records of all that takes place on the bridge shows Kirk *not* pressing the red alert button before jettisoning the pod. He is then accused of perjury and culpable negligence, because his own report differs from the computer records. Kirk is offered an "out" by Commodore Stone by pleading exhaustion. However, Kirk is certain that he followed procedures—no matter what the computer shows—and opts for a trial.

The prosecuting attorney, Lt. Areel Shaw, is an old flame of Kirk's who wants to see him win. She recommends Samuel T. Cogley as his defense attorney. He is eccentric to the point that he actually uses books instead of computers to prepare his case.

Lt. Shaw presents what appears to be an airtight case using the computer records as evidence. Kirk's lawyer, Cogley, has no questions and does not cross-examine. When the presiding officer asks him if he is relinquishing that right, Cogley asks Captain Kirk to take the stand. A visual record of the incident unfortunately backs the prosecution's assertions. Spock cannot believe Captain Kirk would be so negligent, and therefore concludes that the computer must somehow be faulty. He plays a few games of chess to test his theory. Since Spock himself programmed the computer for chess, it would be impossible for the computer to lose. However, Spock *does* win several games against the computer, and so concludes the programs have been altered.

Finney was the records officer on the *Enterprise*, and only he, Kirk, and Spock are able to alter the ship's computer programs. The attorney, Cogley, suggests that Finney is *not* dead, and that he altered the computer in an act of revenge over the reprimand he believed ruined his career. In this way, he'd ruin Kirk's career. They conclude that Finney must be hiding on the ship. After removing all the crew, a handful of people on the bridge amplify the sounds on the ship so they can hear all heartbeats. They eliminate themselves one by one using a device for that purpose, and the only one left, Finney's, is located on B deck in engineering. He is now trying to "kill" the ship by damaging it, but Kirk repairs the damage after subduing an enraged and bitter Lt. Commander Finney.

55

The ego is like a child living inside each of us with an agenda of its own. It wants recognition, attention, and gratification. When it gets the upper hand, feeling neglected and unfulfilled, it can take over common sense, altruism, or any other positive emotional response and quite literally drive us insane. Most of us can admit to temporary insanity when we lose sight of a higher way and choose to indulge our immature and needy egos, but if you find yourself plotting revenge against someone, watch out.

Deception for Advantage

Court-Martial shows us that when we have a focused agenda, we can and will use deception to achieve our ends. Deception is also the dominant theme in *The Enterprise Incident,* but instead of ego-driven madness being the force behind it, *pretending* to be insane is the deception. This is a rare episode in which Spock is in a romantic mode. He finds himself sincerely attracted to a female Romulan commander. His overwhelming loyalty is to the captain, of course, but he does regret that he will have to deceive the lovely Romulan commander.

The Romulan commander believes Spock's loyalty is with her, so when she is trying to find out if Kirk's entrance into the neutral zone was deliberate, she believes what Spock tells her, trusting that Vulcans are incapable of lying. She does not know he is half human.

Kirk then uses the deception of being exhausted and mentally and emotionally unstable to draw attention away from their primary purpose, which is to get the Romulan cloaking device. The old dilemma of how truthful we must be is an eternal moral question, from situations in which we don't want to hurt others' feelings all the way to problems of espionage, where the safety of millions is at stake. It is not my purpose here to analyze this dilemma, but the episode portrays the apparent necessity of keeping secrets and using deception under certain circumstances. Captain Kirk did not even tell his closest colleagues of his plans until it was over, so that his "insanity" would be believable. And as much as we are intrigued by Spock's romantic attraction to the Romulan commander, who is, after all, the enemy, we are also relieved to know that in that regard he was not being deceptive.

Murderous Rage

Star Trek had its own "Jack the Ripper" personified through the episode, *Wolf in the Fold.* The idea of occupying bodies reappears here, but the theme is rage against women. Passion that leads to murder is also covered in *A Private Little War* and to some extent in *Journey to Babel,* where greed and opportunism are the motives for murder.

In *A Private Little War,* a virtual smorgasbord of human frailties is displayed. There we have the prime directive being disobeyed again, along with drugs, betrayal, greed, and seduction. Here's one for Greenpeace. A happy, simple way of life is ruined by one set of people wanting to control the others and doing so with weapons far in advance of their civilization. It clearly shows the wisdom of the prime directive of not interfering in the development of any civilization.

Kirk had been here before and knew the leader of one group, Tyree. The Klingons had been there since Kirk's visit, arming the opposing group with advanced weapons, rendering Tyree's people impotent. It is a quandary for Captain Kirk, who has to weigh alternatives. Once again, he disobeys the prime directive and arms Tyree's people with weapons matching the opposing side, which he says is "putting a serpent into the Garden of Eden." Note that Kirk could have over-reacted and armed the vulnerable group with sufficient force to defeat the other side. Instead, he chooses only to restore the balance that existed before the Klingon intrusion.

We all face moral dilemmas. Do we defend ourselves by killing those who would kill us? Do we "turn the other cheek?" Do we save the mother or the child? Do we retaliate for our loss of 3,000 in an attack by killing more than 100,000 of another country's innocent people? Does war really bring peace?

Obsessive behavior fueled by rage and guilt is truly overwhelming in two *Star Trek* dramas: *Obsession* and *The Doomsday Machine.*

It is Stardate 4202.9 when the *Enterprise* finds out about a doomsday machine. A ship, the *Constellation,* is sending out a distress signal when the *Enterprise* comes upon it. They find an entire solar system destroyed, with only debris where there had been seven planets a year before. Now they see there is another system that has been destroyed with only two planets left. Nearby is the *Constellation* with apparently no one alive on board. It is drifting in space. Beaming over, they find Commodore Matt Decker, alive but in shock. He had beamed his crew down to a hospitable planet when it was immediately destroyed by what he called "the monster from hell." They speculate it is a robot weapon, a "doomsday machine," sent from another galaxy countless years ago to intimidate but not intended to be used.

After Decker transfers to the *Enterprise,* they encounter the

57

machine, and it begins pursuit, attacking and damaging the transporter. Kirk, Scott, and a crewman are still on the *Constellation* repairing what they can. But the machine changes direction and heads toward populous Rigel, ignoring both ships. This does not sit well with Commodore Decker, who wants to avenge his crew and destroy the machine. Since he outranks everyone on the *Enterprise*, he assumes control of the ship and issues orders to attack the "monster." This gets the machine's attention, which causes it to turn and engage in battle.

Kirk, meanwhile, has managed to get a visual on the screen of the *Constellation,* so he can see the battle being fought. Firepower just bounces off the machine with no damage, while the *Enterprise* is sustaining major damage and being held in a tractor beam, which is pulling it slowly inside the monstrous killer. Spock threatens to relieve Decker on the grounds of mental illness, since his is a suicide mission.

When the *Constellation* is repaired enough to maneuver and has phaser power, Kirk moves to distract the machine by firing on it. Communication is also restored, so Kirk orders Decker to be relieved. While being taken to sick bay for observation, he breaks free, steals a shuttlecraft, and rams it down the machine's maw. Commodore Decker felt guilty not perishing with his crew, so this was what he wanted. But sensors register a slight drop in power coming from the machine.

When the transporter is operational, all but Kirk are beamed back to the *Enterprise.* Kirk plans to drive the *Constellation* into the mouth of the machine and beam back to the *Enterprise* at the last minute. He sets a 30-second-delay detonation device for engine overload. Even though the transporter is not wholly reliable, Kirk is successful in killing the monster weapon this way and beams back on board in time.

We are already on the way to building "doomsday machines." We have drones that take photos and fire rockets and do many other things from a safe distance. It is a matter of time, and when we are successful, it is entirely possible that a robot weapon can get lost and wander all over the universe. Even now in Iraq there are weapons in use that fire when triggered by motion detectors rather than soldiers' fingers on the triggers. So what's next?

58

The root of obsession is the belief that we can control a situation, or if in the past, that we *should have* been able to. This can produce guilt if we feel it was our fault that we didn't control an outcome. The problem is that we can't change the past, no matter what we should have done, and also, in reality, we can't control anything or anyone but ourselves.

Guilt is also a waste of time, since we cannot undo the past other than making amends as best we can and then moving on. But tell that to someone who is obsessed with guilt and just cannot forgive himself. It harms the one caught in it and possibly leads to further wasted emotion and ineffective performance as we observe in the episode called *Obsession*.

Eleven years earlier, Captain Kirk had hesitated before firing at a cloudlike creature which ultimately killed 200 crewmen and the captain on board the USS *Farragut*. Kirk blamed himself for those deaths, feeling that if he had fired instantly, he would have killed it. It haunted him so much that on this stardate, 3619.2, as he and four others are collecting a specimen of a rock that is twenty times harder than diamonds, he immediately recognizes the scent of the cloudlike creature when it comes close to the landing party—a sweet scent, like honey. Within a short time two crewmen are dead, victims of this cloud killer. All the red corpuscles in their bodies are gone. A third crewman is gravely ill and perishes later.

Although the *Enterprise* is supposed to be meeting the USS *Yorktown* on an urgent mission, they remain in orbit around Argus X, because Captain Kirk is intent on killing this creature. He is obsessed.

On board is the son of the deceased captain of the *Farragut*, Ensign Garrovick. Kirk asks if he would like to help destroy the creature that killed his father, and the son readily agrees. When a landing party goes after the cloud, Garrovick hesitates this time to shoot on seeing it, and two more crewmen are attacked. The ensign is relieved of his duties and confined for this hesitation.

Captain Kirk is so consumed with this quest that he is not taking medicine to the Theta 7 Colony via the USS *Yorktown*, with whom they are to rendezvous. Dr. McCoy and Spock are threatening to declare him unfit to command because of his obsessive behavior.

The cloud moves out into space, with the ship in pursuit at a higher speed than it can maintain safely. But when the cloud turns and attacks by coming in through the ship's ventilation system, they realize it is indeed an intelligent being with deliberate intent. Shooting at it does no good. Therefore Kirk realizes that his shooting at it years earlier would have made no difference either. But they do learn that the cloud has no liking

59

for anti-matter. Garrovick is released, and together they bait the creature with blood and destroy it by detonating an explosion of anti-matter.

At the base of obsession is control—a feeling that one should be able to *make* something be the way one wants it, whether it is to make someone feel a certain way or do a certain thing or to change a situation, making it different from what it is. Since we can control nothing but ourselves, it is a waste of time and energy.

In a book I read long ago, whose title I don't recall, I encountered a sparkling nugget of advice about how to effect change in others, if it can be done at all. It explained that we all have game rules that we follow with one another. We get used to our intimate relationships and know what buttons to push to get what we want. If the game is not proceeding as you would like, the thing to do is to step outside the rules and respond differently. For instance, if you have a child who does a negative thing repeatedly, and your response has always been the same— say, getting angry—then to change the behavior, you stop "getting angry" and instead do something else. Maybe you could sit down and have a talk or ignore it completely. It doesn't matter what you do as long as it is different and not harmful. The people you wish to change will usually push your buttons harder to make you go back to the game rules they are used to. If you stick with it, they are forced to change *something* just to establish new rules. This is not changing the other person as much as it is changing the dynamics of the relationship, which breaks old patterns and makes way for change, which will ultimately be an agreement on new dynamics between you. Hopefully, it will be for the better.

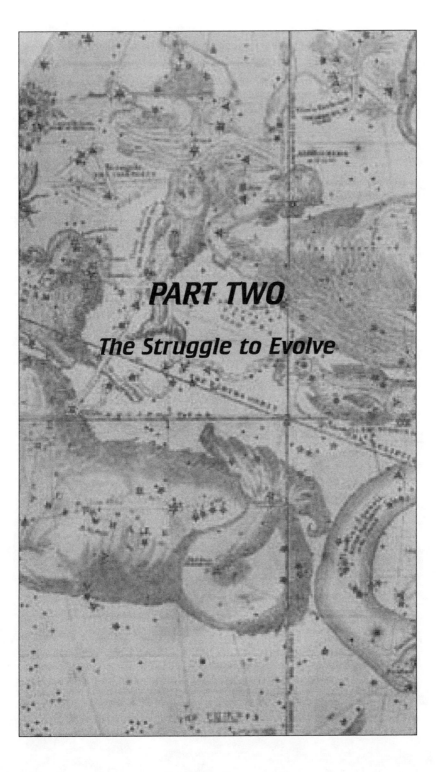

PART TWO

The Struggle to Evolve

CHAPTER FIVE

Misuse of Power and Control

I hope our wisdom will grow with our power, and teach us,
that the less we use our power the greater it will be.
~Thomas Jefferson

The litany of our sins reviewed by the episodes in Part 1, telling us where we have been, provides an overview of where we are in our evolution. It is a bleak picture. Left to ourselves, would we improve at all? I wonder. With the advent of New Age philosophies in the Sixties and later, with other enlightening insights like the material in *A Course in Miracles*, a better understanding of quantum physics, as offered by Gary Zukav in *The Dancing Wu Li Masters*, and even *Star Trek*, our vision expanded sufficiently to accept concepts that we might have brushed off earlier as weirdness or nonsense. The ideas and philosophical insights shown to us through these media laid the groundwork for later acceptance so that we could mature and grow into our next evolutionary stage—understanding that the soul's mind is the master of everything, and that *choice* is the writer of our life scripts, indeed, the creator of our entire personal reality.

One of the first consequences of spiritual expansion is heightened sensitivity, which when carried to high levels becomes what is commonly regarded as psychic or healing ability. This gives the mind control over matter. Jesus, himself, demonstrated this ability and told us we could also do what he did, and even greater things. If we truly believe in Christian teachings, why is it so far-fetched that humans can do the amazing things shown us on *Star Trek* and also demonstrated by other enlightened souls? But with great power comes great responsibility. It is so easy and tempting to misuse uncommon abilities. *Star Trek* dealt with this theme in many episodes, and we could view them as dramas showing mankind's struggle to evolve to a point where we make better and wiser choices.

As we develop psychic, telepathic, and telekinetic ability, it is inevitable that some people will be ahead of others and have an advantage. Evolution demonstrates this inequity of ability as some of us concentrate on spiritual development while others do not. In *Star Trek*, some alien societies were ahead of us metaphysically and scientifically, as were selected individuals who seemed to be singled out for the bestowal of powerful gifts. Some just showed up in the dramas already having supernatural powers, but from where or how we did not know. However, it is lonely when one is exceptional and others are not, and it is tempting to use, even misuse, one's special powers. This is one of the lessons about choice. Do we use power to force others to our will, or do we use it to better other people's condition? It is hard to gain genuine friends if you are different. It cannot be forced, as Charles Evans found out in *Charlie X*.

It is Stardate 1533.6 when the *Enterprise* meets with the cargo vessel *Antares* to receive a passenger, Charlie Evans, who is the only survivor from a crash on Thasus 14 years before. He was raised by Thasians, who are non-corporeal beings, and now needs to find others of his own kind. Charlie has never even seen a human female, so complete has been his isolation. He is now 17 and actively interested in the opposite sex. He becomes fixated on the first woman he encounters, Yeoman Janice Rand.

At first we get a hint of his supernatural powers when he is able to give Yeoman Rand a rare gift that he materializes from nowhere. Then he does impossible card tricks and causes other things to "happen" when he wishes—like Uhura losing her voice when he doesn't like her singing. However, Captain Kirk has to confine him when, in anger, he causes a crewman to disappear. Later, when Yeoman Rand rebuffs him, Charlie causes her to disappear too. Sadly, he cannot understand why everything he does is wrong in gaining others' affection and favor.

Later in the trip, the *Antares* contacts the *Enterprise* to warn them about Charlie, but he destroys their ship during the transmission. No one is a match for Charlie, and he soon assumes command of the *Enterprise* so it will go to Colony Alpha Five, as he wants it to. No one dares interfere with him.

Suddenly a Thasian vessel approaches, and a shimmering specter of a head appears on the bridge explaining that Charlie must return to Thasus since, with his special powers, he would never be able to assimilate with other humans. He had been

63

given the gift so that he could survive on the planet so alien to him, but it would be most detrimental to others if he used it among his own species. He disappears while begging to stay.

Not only do people evolve unevenly in spiritual development, acquiring new skills such as psychic ability, but also we evolve unevenly in intelligence. To paraphrase a recent TV show line, "Be glad you're not a genius; they lead lonely lives." (*Law and Order: Criminal Intent.*) Anyone who is different in *any* way is often perceived as a threat to those who do not understand or who feel inferior.

My teen years could have come out of the movie *Grease*. I wore the cinch belts, neck scarves, and crinolines under my skirts. I was a typical "Sandy." One dared not be different. I learned one huge lesson in the Fifties: don't be smart if you're a girl and want dates. My friends kept telling me to "play dumb," that boys like dumb girls that make them feel smarter. I made A's and B's, but that didn't get me dates. I used to be proud of academic achievement, but not when it threatened the all-important need to be accepted and sought after by the opposite sex. I learned to be self-effacing and to keep the grades secret. This dumb act became such a habit—meaning I was so unaware of it—that in the Seventies an employer said to me once, "You know, you seemed really stupid at first, but I swear, I think you may be close to being a genius." Naturally, that was an exaggeration, but I was shocked to discover my old ruse was still active.

We invite people to treat us as we teach them to, just as *A Course in Miracles* explains. Even now, I catch myself acting like an innocent dumb blond stereotype from time to time. You've heard motivational teachers saying, "Act as if, and you will become it"? It is true. Remember Sandy completely changed her persona at the end of *Grease* to please Danny and vice versa. It happens all the time. We just choose different roles to play and lose our authentic selves in the process. What a waste it is to be someone you are not—to disown possibly the very best part of yourself.

This brings us back to Charlie in *Charlie X*. He wanted to be important to Yeoman Rand and also make friends on the ship, but his authentic self, with his supernatural powers, was not acceptable. Not only was he a perceived threat but he did not make wise choices in how he used his gifts. Unfortunately, he did not have time to familiarize himself with the mores of the group, so he blundered his way through using his will to punish culprits if he was offended. This is the other end of the spectrum of

64

trying to fit into a group—to control the group with fear instead of conforming to it. This is what bullies do. It is guaranteed to get attention.

Other episodes that made this point were *The Squire of Gothos* and *Who Mourns for Adonais?* In the former, we get a glimpse of the future when or if we are able to be points of light and can manipulate matter at will. What would little children be like in a world such as that? How would they play?

The *Enterprise* is going through a void in space when it comes upon an uncharted planet. The ship cannot seem to avoid the planet, which moves as they do, and then suddenly Kirk and Sulu disappear from the bridge. Instead of voice communication, when they try to make contact, they get script in old English on a screen.

The planet is most inhospitable atmospherically to humans, so a landing party beams down in survival gear. They are amazed to find it isn't necessary when they arrive. Communicators do not work there, however. In short order, they discover a castle and go inside. *(A likeness of the "salt vampire" is in a niche.)* Kirk and Sulu are there in suspended animation, and the castle is decorated in Elizabethan style. Trelane, the master of the house, is suddenly playing the harpsichord for his guests, and he releases Kirk and Sulu. He is interested in Earth's history and could not resist having the passing ship's crew as his guests. The only thing is, he is about 700 years behind the times and makes other small mistakes in replicating a place he thought his guests would find familiar and appreciate. For instance, the fire gives off no heat from the fireplace, and the food has no flavor!

Kirk humors him while trying to find a vulnerable place to end the charade. He thinks there is a machine behind a mirror and shoots it. This stops things enough to enable them to go back to the ship.

But Trelane is not done. He brings Kirk back to a "court" where he is the judge and sentences Kirk to hang. Kirk convinces him that there is no sport in that, and challenges him to a one-on-one fight. Kirk and Trelane go outside to duel with swords, although Kirk has no sword, and while engaging in that exercise Trelane's parents interfere.

65

It turns out that Trelane is a child of another species who can make planets out of nothing and create whatever he wishes at will, including his own character.

Most analyses of this episode consider it a light-hearted and fun drama with nothing particularly weighty about it, and for the most part it is. But the misuse of power permeates the whole story. Trelane, the Squire of Gothos, manipulated an entire starship crew to do whatever he wished, and there was no evidence the game would ever end if the parents had not stepped in. This can take on many levels of meaning, from how we empower our children to take over our lives until we have no control, to the manipulation that can occur when anyone has the advantage. The essential point is the almost desperate attempt on Trelane's part to "entertain" his guests and have "fun" with them. He is trying to do this by providing what *he* has decided they would like and forcing it on them. Ergo, the inherent loneliness of one who is more gifted than others and misuses it.

In line with this same theme, the episode entitled *Who Mourns for Adonais?* addresses the sadness of wanting worship, love, and companionship while having great power, but being unable to acquire it through strength of will.

Without getting into the details of the story, we again see an attempt to force love and acceptance from people through manipulation drawn from special power. We cannot help but sympathize with these entities who are ultimately alone. However, the key thing is the *misuse* of these special gifts. In each case, they chose to use force to subjugate people, when they could have chosen to use their abilities in a more noble fashion.

There is inevitably a time in our evolution when various emerging traits are new, unexplored, or in the hands of immature people who have not learned to use them—such as muscle mass in a young man who has not learned to control his passions and doesn't know how much damage he can do.

We are becoming aware of such a time now. The power of the mind to create whatever it gives the most attention, passion, and emotion to was always there. We just never realized *how* we were creating our own dramas from moment-to-moment. The element of choice hadn't yet entered in. Without most of us knowing how to use the power in a positive and productive way, we continuously stay in our ruts and circumstances by default because we keep complaining about them or we keep thinking about, and giving creative energy to, what we *don't* want, thereby creating more of the same. It may take more *time* to manifest the things we think about than, say, Trelane required, but the results are just as inevitable. It is a good thing currently, though. Imagine how chaotic things would be if all our thoughts were made tangible in seconds. We are not ready for that kind of ability. It would be like giving guns to children.

Power for Control

When power is used simply for the sake of control, for entertainment or curiosity, especially when it causes loss of life, it is especially heinous. *The Savage Curtain* is one such episode.

The *Enterprise* is making a last orbit around the planet, Excalbia, when they detect carbon-based entities—improbable on a planet that seems to have nothing but a molten lava surface. They are suddenly scanned by a source on the planet, and just as suddenly, an image of Abraham Lincoln hovering in space appears on the viewer. He says he is the real Lincoln and wants to board the ship.

Since scanners show him to be authentic, he is beamed aboard and given full presidential honors with dress uniforms. However, just before he is beamed aboard, for a split second, the scanners show him to be "living rock," a perplexing curiosity. Lincoln invites Kirk and Spock to beam down to the surface of the planet, and they oblige, although Scott and McCoy protest. Once there, they discover that tricorders and weapons are left behind and their communicators are useless. Abruptly, Surak, considered history's greatest Vulcan, as the one who brought peace to his planet, manifests. He appears to be, and insists that he is, real.

A nearby rock begins to move and comes alive, identifying itself as Yarnek. It is speaking their language, and explains that the inhabitants of the planet, rock-like entities, learn from dramatic presentations they create. In this case, they want to observe which is stronger, good or evil. They have brought together Kirk, Spock, Lincoln, and Surak for the "good" team, and then introduce the "evil" team: Zora (an evil scientist), Genghis Khan (an Earth menace), Colonel Green (a deceptive Earth murderer), and Kahless (a ruthless Klingon). It is a battle to the death, and if they do not participate in the battle, Yarnek will destroy the *Enterprise*.

After plots and deceptions, what is left of the "evil" team flees at the first indication of loss, so the "good" team is declared the winner, after which Spock and Kirk are returned to their ship.

67

It is fascinating that the alien who is orchestrating this evil is portrayed as a rock. What could be more unfeeling and insensitive? Also, a rock is not malleable. It remains unchanged and constant for long periods, thus portraying the impenetrable conscience of those who perpetuate using living beings for their own purposes.

We cringe when we see such a pointless and cold-hearted practice of using people simply as a learning exercise. Yet, it is a method we employ constantly in the way we use animals in laboratories and people in experimental drug testing, during which they can, and often do, lose their lives for learning purposes. Even though much of the human drug experimentation is voluntary, it is also true that many are misled about the dangers involved. It is a deliberate misuse of power—especially regarding innocent, powerless animals, who can do nothing to save themselves.

We need to remember the atrocities committed during WWII, when Jews were used experimentally, sterilized, or otherwise physically violated by doctors of the Third Reich. Even their body parts were used for mundane manufacturing purposes during the Holocaust. The horror we are capable of inflicting when we hold a little power over others is heart wrenching.

Who could be more vulnerable, for example, than mentally ill patients who trust their doctors will do what is best for them. Indeed, society trusts these doctors will do their best to be a healing influence. In *Dagger of the Mind,* an unscrupulous doctor takes outrageous advantage of his position to control inmates and even his assistant.

In this episode, a machine is used to erase memory, which is then "rewritten" with suggestions from the operator of the machine. These suggestions are what the subject really believes to be true from then on. This is the ultimate control—erasing and reprogramming the mind of another person. The episode also brings out the idea that one can die from the loneliness of an empty mind.

We might question why a person would die just from having no thoughts. We know that the mind is a deep and constant wellspring of unconscious thinking. It is never still. We are very seldom in the present moment, since we are usually reviewing memories or making up dramatic scripts for our lives. One of our spiritual goals in life is to learn to live in the moment without judgment or expectation—to just *be.* But if one is not conscious of doing this, then emptying the mind of all thought and memories, leaving nothing behind, could indeed be an excruciating experience. Perhaps it *would* be deadly.

68

This might be an example of a future version of a pre-frontal lobotomy—a way to control minds without working to heal them. The power this puts in the hands of a few is awesome and the implications mind-numbing. We saw a version of this in the film *The Manchurian Candidate*, whereby a man was so controlled through hypnotic suggestion that he even murdered his beloved wife.

Wherever control is more important than the spiritual dimension, there will be the temptation to use advanced intelligence or special knowledge as a means to control other minds, much as a hypnotist does when he uses his ability to put people "under" (*under* their control?) and suggest behavior to them.

The Huna shamans of Hawaii say that it is dangerous to allow oneself to be hypnotized because the hypnotist has a tie to your subconscious mind, whether he knows it or not, with which he can renew those suggestions and plant new ones at any time. This was the way the subject in *The Manchurian Candidate* was controlled at a distance each time he saw a particular playing card. It was the trigger to put him into a hypnotic state again, during which he received instructions to do despicable things.

Does Power Equate to Being a God?

The first episode of *Star Trek* to air was *Where No Man Has Gone Before*. It is considered episode two, historically, because the pilot, *The Cage*, was supposed to precede it. (However, *The Cage* was shown later, integrated into a larger plot as a two-part episode, *The Menagerie*.) So, the first time the public saw *Star Trek*, it was this episode. It set the stage immediately for some interesting concepts and addressed this issue of what one can choose to do with special psychic ability.

While patrolling the edge of our galaxy on Stardate 1312.4, the *Enterprise* receives a recorded distress signal from a spaceship's recorder. It is from the *Valiant*, missing for almost two centuries. The ship's recorder relays a story of encountering an energy barrier that causes damage to the ship and kills some of the crew. One crewman survives and the story is not coherent after that, but there are frantic requests from the ship's databanks for information on extra sensory perception (ESP), for reasons unknown. Inexplicably, the ship is destroyed, ostensibly by the captain.

The *Enterprise* ventures outside the galaxy to find out what

69

caused the captain to destroy his ship and what others may encounter in future. They come upon the same energy field. While going through it, the ship is damaged and leaves them with only impulse power. Two crew members are knocked out by a beam from the field, Dr. Elizabeth Dehner and Lt. Cmdr. Gary Mitchell, who is the navigator. He is left with glowing silver eyes, and with each hour that passes he gains remarkable abilities. He can control his autonomic reflexes, can diagnose mechanical problems on the ship at a distance, can read at rapid speed, and has photographic recall. He is able to hurt people with energy surges from his fingertips and can read minds.

At a meeting of the ship's officers, it is suggested that the *Valiant* captain waited too long to rid himself of an extraordinary crewman affected like Mitchell, and it was the reason he destroyed the ship. Spock advises killing Mitchell while they still can, but Mitchell is a long-time friend of Captain Kirk's, and so the captain is reluctant to do that. He opts instead to leave him on an uninhabited planet, Delta Vega, where there is an automated station that can also help them repair the ship, since they can obtain lithium crystals there. Mitchell has to be sedated in order to beam him down, being so strong by this time.

The landing party puts Mitchell into a brig on the station. From there he is able to control a cable that strangles a crewman in another room. By that time, Mitchell is declaring himself a god and the others insects. Dr. Dehner is beginning to mutate as well, and the two leave the station and head out onto the terrain of the planet. Kirk follows and overtakes them. Mitchell attempts to kill Kirk with his new powers, but when Dr. Dehner realizes that Mitchell is not going to use his abilities for beneficial purposes, she helps Kirk to overpower him, but is killed in the attempt.

Mitchell mentally digs a grave for Kirk complete with headstone (that says "James P. Kirk" instead of "James T. Kirk"), but in the end Kirk uses a phaser to cause an avalanche, which knocks Mitchell into the grave, covering him with rocks.

Since neither Dr. Dehner nor Lt. Cmdr. Mitchell was responsible for what happened to them, Captain Kirk notes in the record that they died in the line of duty.

70

One of the dangerous side effects of having extraordinary abilities is the sense of entitlement—a "god complex." As Spock mentioned in this episode, the empowered being would have as much in common with his fellow men as we would have with mice or insects.

I went to a dinner party in a small town in Virginia a few years ago. The host was the local magistrate, and guests included the local Sheriff and a Red Cross executive, among others. At the dinner table, the magistrate mentioned some of the annoyances of his office. He referred to the common people he had to deal with every day—the ordinary residents of the town who appeared before his bench—as "maggots." There was no trace of compassion or sensitivity in this person who passed judgment on these citizens every day. We don't even need extraordinary abilities to hold ourselves up as gods, do we? Just a little more power than other people have.

Another dramatization of superior entitlement is the episode *Space Seed*, the one in which we meet Khan, later the subject of the movie, *The Wrath of Khan*. Khan was one of a group of genetically bred superior beings. As Spock observed, though, "Superior ability breeds superior ambition." These superior beings took over the entire earth, according to *Star Trek* history, and ruled absolutely near the end of the 20th century. A spaceship the crew now discovers holds those superior beings who escaped, in suspended animation, when the era ended and their group was largely wiped out. When they are taken out of their suspended state, and we get to know them, we witness the arrogance and contempt they have for those not endowed with their superior strength and intellect. Their observation is that things have not improved much in their absence.

It is a basic human urge to evolve—to become more than who we are. We are always striving. It is what we are here to do, so it is part of our instinct. One of the ways we may choose to do it is by artificial means, such as taking mind-expanding drugs or, in this case, by manipulating genes. Some, in attempting to engineer a better body or mind, forget that we are more than merely genes and bodies. Those are just our temporary outer forms. Evolution comes from the inside. By reaching a higher level of spiritual consciousness, we can consciously improve our condition physically. When we get ahead of ourselves, producing a superior body and intelligence without producing a superior spiritual ethic, we have imbalance of the variety seen in Khan, where his pride in his superiority was a playground for the ego— ego, that is, as described in *A Course in Miracles*.

In *The Gamesters of Triskelion*, we find another example of ego run amok. Here we have superior beings who have no bodies (just brains on life support) and have developed *mind* over the

71

physical, but are at a loss as to how to use it in anything remotely resembling an effort at evolving spiritually. To amuse themselves, they capture other species (on the order of the way we took slaves from Africa) and use them much the way the Romans held games at the Colosseum. They make bets and profit from them.

Left to its own devices, the ego is attracted to heightened emotion and sensation. If mind is not conscious or productive, it needs constant stimulation and amusement. Just as a man died of an empty mind in *Dagger of the Mind*, conversely, these beings find life meaningful only if they have something on which to rivet their attention, but it is coming from *outside* them. They are ignoring the creative potential *within* them. So the society is stagnant, with only games being performed over and over for their amusement. The participants are slaves with no ability to change their circumstances, and as in other episodes they wear painful devices used to punish disobedience.

We look at something like this and consider it only fantasy. Nothing like that here, is there? Well, what is the child prostitution and pornography trade all about? It is selling "amusement" by using slave labor. What about the drug trade buying and selling chemicals that enslave people? What about big business taking advantage of the people who work for them by paying them a wage so low they have to work two or three jobs just to survive? Or businesses that cut hours so that it is just below what is required to supply health insurance and other benefits? The owners and CEOs are enjoying life to the fullest with spectacular salaries and rich benefits in the hundreds of millions per year—far more than they need, while the laborers, who make it *possible* for them to live that way, live painful, stagnant, and desperate lives. The hypothetical "gamesters of Triskelion" are alive and well on planet Earth, wielding power over their slaves just as effectively as though they had pain devices on their necks, like the iron "collars" on the necks of the African slaves.

Another episode involving entities deriving pleasure from watching violence is *The Day of the Dove*. Here, an alien non-corporeal being feeds off the energy of violence between crew members on the *Enterprise* and helps instigate it by pitting enemies against one another. It has the power to heal wounds instantly so that the wounded or dead person can rise up and fight again. In a feedback loop, violence escalates as it gains more energy from it. Finally, when Kirk and others figure out the source of all the violence, they deliberately laugh, joke, and generate good feelings. The creature, not getting its "feed," abandons ship.

Metaphysically, this episode is a revelation. I have several friends who often say, "I am not giving that any energy," meaning they will not feed something and invest it with energy to allow it growth. I use the expression myself. It is a law that whatever you feed will expand and grow. What you do not feed will wither and die. This is as true on a mental and energetic level as it is on the physical. In fact, the energetic level *causes* the physical—whether it is an action we take or an object we create. We know that in a group we will have a heightened sense of emotions that are shared. This is why people will commit acts in a mob they would never do while alone.

A friend of mine visited a Pentecostal church at a member's invitation and experienced an amazing phenomenon. She said that when the congregation's chanting and collective worship reached a certain point, she felt a great wave of energy arise from the people and sweep all around them and she felt caught up in it. It isn't that this proves the congregation is "holy" or in any way better or worse than any other group. It is a natural phenomenon that we all can duplicate if we can get enough energy emanating from a group to cause it.

We all are energy, and all materialization of matter is a result of mental and emotional energy and vibration. We create what we focus on with the most intense emotion. If we do not focus on something with emotion, we do not create it. It is dead to us—non-existent. Void. Seth, in Jane Robert's book, *Seth Speaks*, calls our thoughts and emotions the "blueprints" upon which we build our material reality.

Survival and Extinction

That Which Survives could have been included in the list of episodes involving ancient computers left behind to run things, except that the computer in this story isn't controlling a society. It isn't for that purpose. It is a computer left at an outpost to welcome emissaries of their own civilization and to repel intruders. But the race is long-since extinct, so emissaries will not be coming. However it does project a holographic image, which appears real and which kills anyone it considers an intruder. The unique thing is the image's reluctance to do it, suggesting it was programmed by a compassionate and sensitive person. The programming was a necessary evil in the eyes of its creator.

There are two other "survivor of a species" stories that

73

compare to this. One, *Wink of an Eye*, features a few last survivors of a planet on which the males became sterile because of the water, which also raised their metabolism so high they cannot be seen by humans. They sound like buzzing insects. By putting some of their water in Kirk's coffee, he is raised to their metabolism and is becoming invisible to his crew, who appear to him to be barely moving. These aliens know that the higher metabolism will age the humans quickly and they will die, but they are willing to use the men anyway to repopulate their planet. The two females of the group are there to copulate.

They are returned to their planet when the scheme is discovered, but we wonder if the repopulation plan worked. After all, in one scene Kirk is putting his boots back on after being alone for a while in his quarters with Deela, the alien who had her eye on him.

In *The Lights of Zetar*, another species tries to survive by intruding on another's free will. Mira Romaine is on her first Federation assignment—to supervise the transfer of the latest equipment to Memory Alpha, the Central Library of the United Federation of Planets—a planetoid specifically designated for that purpose. She is taken over by "lights" in a storm, which also destroys the library. These lights are the collective life energy of the remainder of a race of people whose planet, Zetar, had died. They have been looking for a host for a millennium.

Alarmed when they discover that her brainwaves are matching the waves of the invading entity(s), the *Enterprise* officers put her into a pressure chamber, where the entity is driven out, since it is not used to high pressure.

Some of these episodes may seem like pure fiction, but if I had not witnessed this kind of abduction of a mind and body as I did when my friend's son was taken over by a deceased entity, I would have found it hard to believe. Ruth Montgomery wrote of advanced entities taking over people's bodies, with their permission, in her book, *Strangers Among Us*, where she speaks of advanced souls coming to carry on the work of ushering in a new age and using the adult body of someone who wants to leave it. She called them "walk-ins." After my personal experience, I'm not so inclined to dismiss this as rubbish anymore. But in her book, these people are not living stagnant and non-productive lives. Nor do they reveal who they are. They are here to do a job and do it anonymously—or rather in the persona of the body they have occupied. As far as others know, that person is still him or herself. Some people, who are quick to tell you about it, and who don't seem to be doing anything productive, claim to be walk-ins, but the non-productivity would arouse my suspicions.

I met someone in California whose roommate was being "possessed" by a spirit who claimed to be her soulmate. They were so obsessed with this phenomenon they hardly went anywhere or did anything. It consumed their very lives. One must be careful of dabbling in these arenas. Just as deception is a constant here in our perceived "real" world, it also is in some parts of the spirit world.

Many years ago, in the late Seventies, I was invited to spend an afternoon visiting a couple of teachers in a large eastern city. They were instructors at one of the area's most prestigious schools. It soon became apparent that they were consumed with their Ouija board and an entity they contacted each day called "Teddy." I was fascinated by the information they were gleaning, which was mainly personal to them, but I had no interest in it myself.

A few days later, they called me and said that Teddy wanted me to make contact, for there was an important message. I didn't have a Ouija board, so I called a friend who had one and she came over with it to help me communicate with Teddy. Instantly, when we started, the planchette (the plastic pointer) zapped around the board with no help from us. We just had our fingers suspended over it, not actually touching it. This scared the heck out of me. I had not revealed any names to my friend, and I had assumed that Teddy was spelled that way and was male. Much to my surprise, the board said it was "Tedi" and that it was female. That is how I *know* it was not from my subconscious. Since neither of us touched the planchette, we certainly could not have been pushing it ourselves. But when the manipulative spirit said to come back tomorrow for the important message, that was it for me. I wasn't about to waste time daily on a board. Apparently, there is no shortage of disembodied spirits ready and available to live vicariously through us or amuse themselves by keeping up a running "conversation."

Stealing Identity Again

75

Whom Gods Destroy is a rich, multi-layered episode. The principal character, Garth of Izar, a brilliant former Starship captain, is an inmate of an asylum on Elba II where the *Enterprise* is delivering a new medicine. The colony's governor, Donald

Cory, meets them, but he turns out to actually be Garth. The real Donald Cory is in Garth's cell, disheveled and beaten. Prior to his incarceration there, Garth learned a technique called cellular metamorphosis, which was intended to regenerate damaged cells, but he distorted its use to assume the identity of anyone he chose by changing appearance and becoming a replica, just as the Salt Vampire did.

Marta, the blue-skinned dancer in this drama, also an inmate, tries to seduce Kirk into revealing secret passwords, which would enable Garth to get on the *Enterprise* and take over as a duplicate of Kirk, but she ends up trying to kill him. Spock explains that it is her way of guaranteeing the fidelity of lovers—by killing them. (Garth destroys her in one of his insane rants.) Garth, as do many of those who see themselves as superior, whether insane or not, wants to be called "Lord Garth" and insists on a coronation. He is, in the end, subdued, and the new medicine is highly effective, essentially putting him on the path to recovery. He remembers none of the events that had occurred.

Certainly, the writers of this episode were not thinking about cloning and the questions of ethics. But it is fascinating that Garth had learned cell metamorphosis (no matter how far-fetched that concept may be), first as a healing technique to relieve suffering, and then misused it for his own ends—identity theft. Imagine the ramifications if and when we can clone ourselves at will and the new crimes that could arise as a result. Hopefully, by that time we will have evolved past the need to deceive.

It is clear that we cannot escape who we are. Even though Garth had the appearance of other people, and even sounded and acted like them outwardly, he could not control revelations of his character. As Allan Asherman in his *The Star Trek Compendium* rightly points out, one of Garth's mistakes, when he was duplicating Spock, was to point his phaser directly at Captain Kirk while speaking with him—something the real Spock would never have done.

The compassion shown the mentally ill in this future time is encouraging. Garth is treated respectfully after the medicine is administered because, after all, he is ill and wasn't really himself when he was ranting about being the "Lord of the Universe."

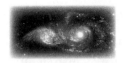

CHAPTER SIX

Evolving Conscience

When will our consciences grow so tender that we will act to prevent human misery rather than avenge it?
~ Eleanor Roosevelt

Isn't it fascinating that we have disputes about whether or not to display the Ten Commandments in public government buildings, but at the same time the majority of those who support it also support avenging the 9/11 attack on the World Trade Center by invading other countries and killing many times the number of innocents who perished in the WTC attack? There does not appear to be the same value placed on *their* lives as is placed on American lives. We are all one. So the value of anyone's life—Christian or Muslim—is equal. If we are one, then when we attack another, we attack ourselves. For good reason, Christianity teaches to treat our neighbors as we would treat ourselves.

What happened to "Thou shalt not kill?" What did "Turn the other cheek" *mean*? Why do you think Jesus told us to "do good to them that hate you" (Matt. 5:44)? It is because hatred produces more hatred, not a solution. To break a cycle, one must find the cause and refuse to give more energy to it in *like kind*. I am mystified when I witness Christians using Scripture from the *Old* Testament to support unconscionable behavior—such as taking "an eye for an eye." This was supposed to have been changed by grace as taught in the *New* Testament. It is common knowledge that Jesus came to *change* the old laws, not to uphold them. He re-enforced the Ten Commandments, however, by making them stricter. *Thinking* of doing something is now the same as doing the deed.

It is a primitive reaction to respond to attack with more

77

attack. It comes from a visceral survival instinct and has nothing in common with spiritual enlightenment. Anyone can fight back. Anyone can love people who are friends and family, but it takes more evolvement and more spiritual muscle to love someone who seeks to obliterate you and your country or race. Love is stronger than hatred and wins every time. If we had spent billions on aid to those impoverished countries, instead of billions on attacking them, how could they hate us? How can you hate someone who is giving you food and medicine?

We do not reach a point by ourselves where we support war or seek revenge. We have examples teaching us love or fear. *A Course in Miracles* tells us that we teach love or fear in every single action. Our reactions to encounters on a daily basis, no matter how innocent, not only teach people how to respond to us but teach people how we view life. If we are fearful, we perceive a world of attack and revenge. If we believe everything is an expression of love, our expectations will be verified.

It is revealing how our inclinations mirror those people we revere and respect. In the early 90s I had a friend who admired a larger-than-life character who lived on a boat. He was anchored nearby taking on supplies, so we went to visit. His nickname was "Bullet Proof Sam" (named changed). There has to be a reason for "bullet proof" to precede your name. I watched my friend's face glowing with hero worship as we listened to "Bullet Proof" tell of his latest exploits on the High Seas.

Personally, I have never encountered a person with a gun unless they were preparing to go hunting or unless I was viewing a gun collection behind a display case. Sam, however, saw guns everywhere. The lady in the boat next to him had one, as did just about everyone in a quarter-mile radius. That dock on that hot, sleepy, sunny day was bristling with gunslingers. He said there was a contract out on him, which was why he had to keep moving and keep his location a secret. I had deep compassion for this poor man. He led such an impoverished life, no matter how much money he had. And my friend? He seemed to have just one annoying fight after another. What else could be expected? He admired force through violence. But like anything else, this is a choice, and it brings us what we expect.

78

Some of the *Star Trek* episodes demonstrated how we can choose which path we will take when presented with options between destructive power and control versus mercy and love. That theme, of course, was constant throughout the series, but in these few the choice was entirely free, not something done through self-defense.

Choosing a Higher Way

Arena is an episode in which there is a demonstration that reverence for right and wrong can be shown by defying an order not consistent with one's conscience.

The *Enterprise*, in pursuit of a predator who destroyed the outpost on Cestus III, inadvertently chases them into Metron space. An unidentifiable power stops and holds both ships motionless, freezing their weapon systems. The two captains, Kirk and a Gorn, a reptilian species, are put on an asteroid to settle their differences. The Metrons tell them that violence is not permitted in their territory, and when one of them has overcome the other, the losing ship will be destroyed. By finding the necessary raw materials on the asteroid, Kirk constructs a cannon and defeats the Gorn, but he tells the Metrons he will *not* kill the reptilian captain, and he requests, when asked, that they not destroy the Gorn ship, either.

A representative of the Metrons materializes and tells Kirk he is surprised to see the advanced trait of "mercy" in humans, and that perhaps there is hope for them—in about 1,000 years. But he observes Kirk and his species to be still half savage.

During the pursuit and before encountering the Metrons, Spock had mentioned that perhaps they should not engage the Gorns in battle because of reverence for life. It would not bring back the dead on Cestus III, he reasoned, to kill the attackers. But it was Kirk who then wanted to destroy them so they would not do damage elsewhere. It makes one wonder if it is because it is easier and more impersonal to destroy a ship from a distance than it is to actually kill one person (or intelligent reptile) in hand-to-hand combat. Or did he not like being *told* he had to kill the Gorn? Whatever, Kirk chose his own way of dealing with the situation when actually ordered to kill.

The tone of the Metrons was parental—not protective parental, but disciplinary. Both factions were treated like children in need of control. This attitude took the glamor out of battle and killing, reducing it to nonsense. The Metrons could also be considered "controllers," but they were merely getting rid of a nuisance in an efficient way, not trying to maintain control for advantage. In fact, they mentioned that their solution for

79

Kirk and the Gorn's dispute was designed to fit their "limited mentality," which is an apt description of the war-like mind. It is a good example of how control and power can be used in a responsible and humane way, just as Kirk's choices demonstrated a sense of conscience and mercy.

These examples of higher choices are so different from episodes like *Charlie X* and *Where No Man Has Gone Before*. In those we saw the extreme negative side of power, but in these a solution is offered—an example of how we can all benefit from higher-minded choices. Many times I've heard people lament the cost in the lives of our children sent off to foreign countries to fight wars they probably do not understand. We even make it a badge of patriotism, calling it the "price of freedom." These people have suggested that the two leaders of the countries, or their individual representatives, get into an arena and fight it out one-on-one to settle their disputes, rather than ravage a country and kill thousands of innocents, including children. In this episode, that is exactly what is done. The two captains alone have the battle.

Perhaps it's in this area of the use of power that choice first becomes important. Few of us, in the heat of emotion or passion, are inclined to consider options. But when the issue is power, we seem to have a little more space to consider what we should do. Kirk, in particular, seems to be responsible in his use of power. He considers his alternatives, and then applies power in a balanced way in order to bring about a good end. Rarely do we see him applying power for selfish ends, or using power to force someone to do something against their will. Compare this use of power with the Klingons, who generally use force without even considering other options. In this sense, Kirk symbolizes an evolving humanity, learning to use its power wisely and constructively, for the good of the whole situation rather than for the short-lived gratifications of aggression, control, and revenge.

Many of the episodes of *Star Trek* set up confrontations between the *Enterprise* and an adversary in which the audience feels the urge to use maximum force against the enemy. We learn from Kirk, often with the advice of fellow officers, the surprising outcomes that are possible when courage and quick wits combine with the *choice* to not misuse power.

Our aggressive feelings are aroused by the episode and then short-circuited by a solution that aggression by itself would never have even looked for. Thus are we gently taught to choose differently. Use power only in the service of all concerned.

"Intelligence" Run Amok

Another instance of choosing a higher course of action can be seen in the episode *Plato's Stepchildren*. Alexander is a dwarf on a planet of normal-sized people. The genetic component that caused his size is also the one that blocks his attainment of the telekinetic power the others developed from eating the native food supply on a planet they colonized centuries earlier— Platonius, named for the leader's hero, Plato. The leader, Parmen (obviously named after the Greek philosopher Parmenides, of the 5th century BC, who was a strong influence on Plato), is gravely ill from a cut. These people can die from a simple infection, and they infect easily. To heal this, they simply hijack a passing ship to obtain a doctor.

These are highly intelligent people who spend their time in contemplation, but some are more powerful telekinetically than others (which is how a leader is selected); the temptation to use their power for status and amusement has seduced them. Poor Alexander has become everyone's slave, since he cannot control anyone. Moreover, the ones who do have such power are merciless at humiliating those who do not, including the officers who have been summoned to help them. When Dr. McCoy develops a drug to give the *Enterprise* officers an accelerated and stronger telekinetic ability than the leader, Parmen, they also offer it to Alexander. He poignantly refuses because he has experienced the negative expression of such power and does not want to be tempted.

We have all heard of specially gifted people who can make objects move with their minds, bend spoons, or do other amazing things. Usually, people suspect there is a trick to it and are not really impressed. Most new theories, such as telekinesis, are not accepted by the public right away. As Schopenhauer said, "All truth passes through three stages. First, it is ridiculed. Second, it is violently opposed. Third, it is accepted as being self-evident." However, as mentioned before, we are on different timetables, with some people far ahead of others. Mike Dooley (www.tut. com) speculates that when there are so many who are evolved in a particular area, it reaches a tipping point, where most everyone is finally in agreement, and new abilities or bodies of knowledge are finally taken for granted. Chiropractic is one such body of

81

knowledge. For many years, it was looked upon with suspicion, but now it is widespread and respected. Another is the idea of the sun being at the center of our solar system. It took a century for that to gain general acceptance.

Mortality for Love

My favorite episode is *Metamorphosis*. It is a love story. No battles, no phasers, just a tale of sacrifice for love. The main character is a cloudlike alien consisting largely of electricity. It takes over a shuttlecraft transporting Nancy Hedford, an Assistant Federation Commissioner, to sick bay on the *Enterprise* because she is suffering a rare and fatal illness. The "cloud" deposits them on the planet Gamma Canaris N. There they find a human who has been marooned for 150 years but looks like he is in the prime of life. He turns out to be Zefram Cochrane, the inventor of warp drive. He had gone into space at age 87 to die there, but the cloud had brought him to that planet, saved his life, and rejuvenated him.

The first thing he notices is the lovely Nancy Hedford, since he hasn't seen a female in a long time, but she is getting weak from illness and is outraged by the detour. Even if she had been well, it is unlikely she would have been interested in Mr. Cochrane, since she has not allowed herself to have a personal life, her career having priority.

This is a story about interracial love, though—or inter-species. When the visitors suggest that the cloud could cure Nancy, since it rejuvenated Mr. Cochrane, they modify a translator to communicate with the alien cloud, which Cochrane calls the Companion. They discover that the Companion is female and is very attached to Cochrane, much like a lover. In the end, the alien Companion takes over the body of Commissioner Hedford, who was about to die. The ultimate sacrifice: the immortal Companion becomes mortal to be with Zefram Cochrane in human form.

The universal translator they used works on a principle that this fable tries to get across—that all cultures have universal themes and ideas. When they all discover that the Companion is actually "in love," Cochrane reacts in what Spock calls "parochial" fashion—disgusted that he allowed that alien thing to crawl all around him, into his mind, and so forth. It reminds us of remarks others have made about interracial relationships. But McCoy says it is "just another life form; you get used to these

82

things." Cochrane's reaction *is* surprising since the two have had a symbiotic relationship for 150 years.

There are two other issues that could be touched on. One is consciousness. We are finding out that everything has consciousness. Scientist Masaru Emoto's book *The Hidden Messages in Water*, offers compelling scientific evidence that we interact with water. He shows photographs of frozen molecules of water taken from different locations and exposed to different environments and emotions. Those samples that are clean and natural have been exposed to positive words or beautiful music and have beautifully formed, colorful, snowflake-like crystal patterns, but those exposed to negative or polluted sources have malformed crystals and are dull by comparison. Even exposure to *written* words affects the outcome. Since our bodies and most of the earth are composed of water, it does not take a genius to deduce what this means. As mentioned earlier, we are connected, and everything we think and feel affects everything else.

Deepak Chopra has said that our bodies react instantly to outside stimuli, such as a beautiful sunset, lovely music or, on the negative side, to disorder and squalor. Beauty isn't a luxury; it's healthy.

All this is really logical. Since subatomic particles respond to thought and emotion, and all molecules are composed of subatomic particles, it is reasonable to conclude that all things are conscious and respond to thought and emotion—everything. That *might* include a cloud-like entity on a distant planet, which can rescue and relate to an old man dying in space.

Another issue we can look at is the particle world of love. In her book *Love Without End: Jesus Speaks*, artist Glenda Green, relating her conversation with Jesus, explains adamantine particles (which are far smaller than any particles so far discovered) as being particularly affected by love, and that the exchange of these particles between those who love each other is healing. This exchange is also behind the phenomenon of people who have lived together a long time beginning to look alike. These particles work on magnetic principles, much like iron filings being attracted to a magnet. Haven't we always said that attractive people have "magnetic" personalities?

When watching *Metamorphosis*, we are struck by how the cloud entity could not heal Commissioner Hedford, but that the commissioner *was* healed as soon as the entity took over her body. Commissioner Hedford on her deathbed overheard

83

the expression of disgust as Cochrane ranted. She could not understand anyone who refused love, even from an alien, since she had never been loved and was regretting having to die before having that experience. If adamantine particles are healing, perhaps it was the love the entity brought to her body that did the healing. In Green's book, Jesus is said to have explained that the woman who touched his robe, and who was healed, did so because she actually touched his love for her, which was the healing agent.

In the Eye of the Beholder

Medusa, in ancient myth, was one of the Gorgons and was once very beautiful. But she bragged to Athena about her beautiful hair and Athena, through jealousy, turned her into a hideous creature with snakes for hair, fearsome fangs, and so ugly that anyone who looked at her turned to stone. When Perseus beheaded her, he had to do it while looking at her reflection in his shield.

In the episode entitled *Is There in Truth No Beauty?* an alien is brought aboard the *Enterprise* from a race aptly called Medusans. They are nearly formless beings, so difficult for humans to behold that the sight of them causes madness. Special visors are used to prevent it. The empathic Dr. Miranda Jones is escorting Medusan Ambassador Kolos (safely secured in a box out of sight) back to his home planet. The Medusans are known for their superb navigational skills as well as having the most sublime thoughts in the galaxy. Helping her is her admirer, Lawrence Marvick, who is jealous of Miranda's attention and dedication to Kolos. Her devotion could be compared to the Shakespearean Miranda in *The Tempest,* who was similarly dedicated to her father, Prospero. (*Star Trek's* character names are always beautifully relevant.)

Naturally, since the Medusan name is based on the mythical snake-haired Medusa, there have to be some victims in this story who look upon Kolos and turn mad. Lawrence Marvick, who is in love with Miranda and doesn't want her to devote her life to Kolos, tries to kill him, but the Medusan opens his box in self-defense, driving Marvick mad. Marvick ends up throwing the *Enterprise* into unknown territory when he takes over the ship in a frenzy and subsequently dies. To return to where they were, Spock has to consult Kolos, an expert navigator, which can only be done with a mind meld. Kolos actually takes over Spock's body and guides the ship back to where it was, but when they

84

break the bond Spock forgets the visor and goes insane. Miranda suspends her own jealousy, caused by Spock's affinity with Kolos, mind melds with him, and saves his life.

The real subject of this episode is an examination of what beauty is. The characters over dinner discuss the ancient Greek idea that if something is beautiful it must be good and vice versa. The title could have been *Is Truth Beautiful?* The theme of beauty versus ugliness is also symbolized through Kirk presenting Miranda with a rose, not once but three times, emphasizing how thorns accompany the rose. We could not help but be reminded of "A rose by any other name would smell as sweet," from Shakespeare's *Romeo and Juliet* and all of the many analogies regarding the necessity of accepting the thorns with the rose.

Miranda is dedicating herself to the ugliest of beings, though she is quite beautiful, moving McCoy at one point to comment, "How can one so beautiful condemn herself to look upon ugliness the rest of her life." Her choice to be a companion to Kolos is a lifetime assignment that precludes other relationships. But this is still unsettled as they board the ship, because the permanency of it depends on her being able to achieve true "oneness" with the Medusan ambassador. We get a glimpse of the source of her jealousy over Spock's ability to bond with the Medusan, when Spock expresses his admiration for Kolos and his envy of her job. When Spock is gone, she fires at Kolos, "What does he see when he looks at you?"—a curious thing to say since she *appears* to be looking at him herself.

Another question the officers ask Miranda is how she can protect her sanity since she is so close to Kolos and could go mad herself if she inadvertently forgot to wear the visor. She brushes this off as ability through training she acquired on Vulcan, but we learn later that she is really *blind,* the ultimate protection, and a garment she wears holds a web of sensors that enable her to "see" as much or more than a sighted person. Further, we find that her choice to sacrifice her life for the Medusan is based somewhat on escaping the emotions of humans, especially one she hates—pity.

Spock appreciates the beauty of the mind, logic, and pure thought, and we get a chance to see how lovely the Medusan is when he expresses himself through Spock. His soliloquy about how lonely humans are, trapped in their flesh and separate from one another, is reminiscent of the remarks the Companion made in *Metamorphosis* when first experiencing what it is to be human.

85

Finally, after achieving a mind meld with Spock, Miranda is able to become one with Kolos and leaves the ship with full appreciation of what Spock saw when he looked at him.

The Power of Choice

All these scenarios involved a choice, and choosing is the most important action any of us can do. Every time we encounter a dilemma in which we have to decide upon a response, we create a new potential outcome for our lives. To every action there is a re-action. Haven't you ever wondered what would have happened if you made different choices? "What if I'd married so-and-so instead of the one I did?" "What if I'd gone to a particular college instead of another?"

The book, *One*, by Richard Bach, presents the idea of parallel lives which are created according to choices we have made. (In this book Bach speaks often about his wife, Leslie Parrish, and her life. She played the part of Carolyn Palamas in the *Star Trek* episode *Who Mourns for Adonais?*, and, incidentally, in that episode she had the most difficult choice of spurning a god, whom she really cared for, to save her shipmates.) In *One*, Bach uses an airplane as his vehicle to go from one scenario to another, depicting the results of various choices he and his wife have made. When he is in those parallel lives, they are just as real as the one he believes he is living, and at times he is frightened about not being able to get back to the one he identifies with. It is like a tour of the roads not taken and what would have happened if they had been.

This question of choice is also explained in *Seth Speaks* by Jane Roberts. The idea is that whenever we are presented with a choice, such as whether to divorce or whether to have an abortion, we "split" into two of ourselves, each one taking the alternative paths presented. Each thinks of itself as the only character in the play and is unaware of the split. Since this possibly happens with every choice made, it means that we'd end up with thousands of different possible "lives" all being lived simultaneously. On the one hand, it is encouraging because our souls would not miss any experiences as a result of choices. However, it boggles the mind regarding how the universe works.

86

Even if this theory is not correct, it is still crucial that we learn to be more mindful of the choices we make. We can choose not to drive when we drink, not to respond with rage when annoyed, and to do a little research about both sides of issues so we can vote for people who have integrity. Choice is really *everything*.

Even choosing what to think about is vital. As mentioned before, whatever we choose to give mental and emotional energy to will become our future. Further, it also displays one's level of evolvement. Base choices to gratify the moment are primitive, but those that enhance life or sacrifice a momentary pleasure for the good of the whole—these lift us all to a higher plane. We are one. We are connected. And every higher choice we make adds love and evolvement to the whole.

CHAPTER SEVEN

Concerns of Society

Society is indeed a contract.... It is a partnership in all science; a partnership in all art; a partnership in every virtue, and in all perfection. As the ends of such a partnership cannot be obtained in many generations, it becomes a partnership not only between those who are living, but between those who are living, those who are dead, and those who are to be born.
~ *Edmund Burke*

Even though some aliens who took human form commented that we had to be lonely in our bodies—isolated from one another—we are nevertheless dependent on society for survival. It would be impossible for us to have any real quality of life if we each had to grow our own food, weave our own cloth, and perform individually all the tasks we need to survive. From tribal times there has always been recognition of co-operative effort for the benefit of the whole.

Further, the group needs leadership. On a spaceship—or any vessel—there is a hierarchal structure necessary so that it will function in an orderly manner. Just as an individual body has a brain to oversee activity, so must the "body" of a society require a designated leader or "head." Even some Christian religions refer to the congregation as the "body of Christ" with Christ as the "head." Dietrich Bonhoeffer expressed this beautifully in his book, *The Cost of Discipleship,* when he said, "...for all are members of His body, the Church. The Church bears the human form, the form of Christ in his death and resurrection." Bonhoeffer was known best for his resistance to Hitler, whom he saw as a leader from hell, and once commented, in justification of the attempted assassination for which he was executed, that it was not wrong to wrest the wheel of a car from the hands of a madman speeding down the autobahn. (I have to suspend judgment on that one, as far as actually killing the madman is concerned.)

In society, the leader ideally keeps the interests of the group uppermost in mind, and if not, the collective members of the society will inevitably revolt—or at least show their displeasure. In the episode *Galileo Seven*, Spock gets command over six members of a team who depart on the shuttlecraft *Galileo* to examine a quasar-like phenomenon. Because of the ionization effect of a storm, instruments on both vessels fail and they lose contact. The shuttlecraft is propelled onto Taurus II, a class M planet. Spock's decisions thereafter appear cold-blooded and heartless to his team, who express their disgust at every opportunity over his "logic."

Captain Kirk does not know where Spock and his team have gone, and without the aid of search instruments, he describes the finding of a needle in a haystack as "child's play," compared to success in locating the *Galileo*. To complicate matters, Galactic High Commissioner Ferris is on board to oversee the delivery of medical supplies to Makus III and is fuming over the delay required to investigate the quasar phenomenon. Thus, two leaders are being challenged: Kirk by Ferris and Spock by his team. Their leadership styles are vastly different, and the complaints are the *opposite* of each other. The members of Spock's landing party complain he is heartless and unfeeling toward his crew—and it does seem that way when he speaks of having to leave one or two behind to make the shuttlecraft light enough to take off—and Ferris is complaining about Kirk taking so much time and effort to rescue his missing crewmen when it looks so hopeless.

Oddly, Spock finally saves the remaining members of the landing party (two had been killed by aliens) through an act of emotional desperation—having the team ignite all the fuel they have left, to make a flare that the *Enterprise* might be able to see. Spock, of course, sees the solution as the only logical alternative, and it works.

Leadership by Birthright

We see different styles of cultural custom and leadership also in *Friday's Child* and *Amok Time*. In *Friday's Child*, the culture on Capella IV admires strength and believes in survival of the fittest. Their people are large, swift, and strong. The Klingons and the Federation both have an interest in mining a rare mineral found on Capella IV and seek an agreement for mining rights. A Klingon representative appears first and believes he has reached a mining agreement before the landing party from the *Enterprise*

89

arrives. When the landing party does get there, a young crewman reacts too swiftly, pulls his phaser upon sight of the Klingon, and is killed by one of the Capellans to protect their Klingon guest. Everyone has to surrender their weapons and communicators when they arrive to show good faith, and the Klingon had already done so; therefore he was unarmed when the crewman pulled his phaser.

The current High Teer Akaar, the leader of the Capellans, is subsequently killed, and his pregnant wife, Eleen, is supposed to submit to being murdered, since she carries the heir to the throne. Kirk, in an effort to save her life, grabs her to save her from the knife coming down upon her back. It is part of this culture that no one touches the wife of a Teer, living or dead. So Kirk, McCoy, Spock, and Eleen are all put under guard for their infractions. They escape, McCoy delivers the baby in a cave, and after the new Teer sacrifices his life so that the Klingon, who had stolen a weapon, can be killed, the infant, Leonard James Akaar (after Dr. McCoy), is named the new High Teer Akaar.

This kind of "heir to the throne" leadership is still part of some governments, even if only as a figurehead. Unfortunately, unless the royal family keeps close touch with the people, a callous disregard for the problems of the society is inevitable.

Star Trek presented a vision of a future global society that is free of most discrimination, one form of which is the caste system, where one is born into the same social level as one's parents. The system is usually so ingrained that there is little hope of rising above one's station. These societies routinely arrange marriages between children before they are old enough to even know what marriage is. In the episode *Amok Time,* we find that Spock has been "married" since the age of seven. When the story begins, he is entering *pon farr,* which any *Star Trek* fan knows is the Vulcan mating cycle. He has to go to Vulcan to fulfill his marriage obligation, but as can be predicted, his chosen wife, T'Pring, has fallen in love with someone else. However, she plots a way out of the final marriage ceremony while still preserving Vulcan customs. The cool, clear logic of T'Pring in making her choice is so fascinating, we cannot help but be impressed. (And we won't give the details, in case any reader hasn't yet seen the episode.)

90

Although *Amok Time* is not a story about a whole society in the strictest sense, it does bring up a common issue that is still a concern and the cause of much turmoil. The argument goes that romantic love is not reliable in the choice of a lifetime commitment and that those who are older and wiser should make those decisions. So some groups, like the fictional Vulcans, use various systems of logic to determine who is best suited as a partner for another. It can be based on family assets, divination, or any of the traditional customs. However, it is done at such a young age, the two have not become who they are ultimately going to be, so when the time comes for the consummation of this lifetime commitment they are usually strangers to each other. Some people even today have committed suicide rather than fulfill such an arrangement.

On the other hand, random, uncommitted reproduction based on casual attraction is hardly the answer either—just as marrying out of romantic love is also not noted for its spectacular, long-term success. Although *Star Trek* raised some of the problems of marriage and child rearing, it did not offer many solutions, and of course it wasn't necessarily *meant* to. The issue was addressed in subsequent series, like *The Next Generation*, when there were families and a ship's counselor aboard the ship. In fact, the idea of having families come along on lengthy assignments was a brilliant solution to many domestic problems, providing the crew with a sense of community and social connectedness.

Overpopulation

The Trouble with Tribbles is one of the most popular episodes, and unquestionably the most amusing. Most people hardly remember the real storyline being about poisoned grain, so taken were they by the cute, trilling little Tribbles. Navigator Chekov adds to our amusement with his ongoing claim that Russia was the inventor of almost everything, including, in this episode, scotch (by an old lady in Leningrad). The rapid reproduction of the Tribbles leads to comments about their eating so much, but producing nothing (except offspring). However, when they are found to be dying in the storage bins of the space station, the poisoning of the grain is discovered, leading to the saving of many lives. In a light-hearted way, the problem of over-population and feeding everyone is highlighted and has much in common with another episode, *The Mark of Gideon*.

Star Trek did not choose names arbitrarily. Some things may have been named in honor of people associated with the show, but more often they were chosen because of association with the topic in the drama. We are told in the Bible that Gideon had 70 sons with many wives and died "in a good old age." (Judges 8:30-

91

32) What better choice of name could one have for a planet that is overpopulated?

We think paradise would mean no sickness, no death, mild temperatures, and abundant food. That is what Gideon is— paradise. Death is virtually unknown, peace reigns supreme, and since reverence for life is so inviolable, there is no birth control. The result? A teeming population, so numerous that no one can be alone. We should be careful what we ask for.

Captain Kirk knows none of this when he is transported to the surface, where he expects to appear in the council chambers of the planet, but instead ends up in a replica of the *Enterprise.* He thinks his crew has disappeared. Then a beautiful young woman called Odona shows up dancing around the open spaces of the empty ship, thoroughly enjoying herself. When Captain Kirk questions her, she mentions that where she comes from, (paraphrased) "There is no place, no house, no mountaintop, no beach where anyone can be alone." They are so crowded that her last remembered location was an arena where everyone was so packed together it was hard to breathe. She claims not to know where she came from, although she is really the daughter of the Gideon councilman, Hodin.

This episode highlights the supposed importance of disease in keeping a population under control, since the whole point of Odona's interaction with the captain is to get herself infected with a disease that had nearly killed Kirk. He still carries it in his blood, and she had volunteered to give her life to help her people by exposing herself to his disease and carrying it back to them. However, when she does fall ill, her life is saved aboard the *Enterprise,* and she then goes back to Gideon to happily infect others.

An Evolved Society

We work hard to progress toward what we call success, in order to live better—however we define a "better life." One of the marks of a healthy society is the happiness and wellbeing of the majority of its citizens. This implies an environment in which everyone has freedom to expand and to grow.

Star Trek gave us a vision of a society that created the conditions under which a person could aspire to use talents to optimal ability. Food, money, and education were not an issue. Basic survival needs were met automatically so that citizens could focus on what mattered: participation in society with the talents they had to contribute to the whole. It seems so simple, so why is it so difficult in reality?

In his series of books, *Conversations with God*, Neale Donald Walsch in Book Two tells us that society will not be viable for everyone until we understand *"...the ultimate truth: that what you do to others, you do to yourself; what you fail to do for others, you fail to do for yourself; that the pain of others is your pain, and the joy of others your joy, and when you disclaim any part of it, you disclaim a part of yourself."*

This is also taught in *A Course in Miracles*. We truly are one. But it might be easier to understand if it's put this way: When a genius is not allowed education, the loss is society's for not tapping that genius and benefiting from what could have been discovered or produced by that person. We could have been quantum leaps ahead in our evolution if we had educated and allowed all our citizens to use their gifts to the best of their ability. Instead, many Einsteins and Edisons have probably died in a war somewhere, or are struggling just to make ends meet, never to express the talent they had to give. The loss is definitely everyone's. As an Edgar Cayce reading said, "Many a Mozart is digging ditches."

CHAPTER EIGHT

Healing

Eventually you will come to understand that love heals everything, and love is all there is.
~ Gary Zukav

Now, in the 21st century, we see our mainstream healing abilities as almost magical. We are used to immunizations, antibodies, and a whole spectrum of drugs that are sometimes questionable, regarding side effects, but also amazing in their curative powers. Yet we are sicker than ever. Our foods are full of toxins, preservatives, and fillers. Sugar, which is never found in nature in as concentrated a form as we consume it, is added to almost everything. Most people over 50 are more concerned about their health than any other subject. With all our wealth and technology, we in the United States are a nation of overweight, sick people.

In *Star Trek*, we are enthralled at the spectacle of healing that is so much more magical, it seems impossible. But the good Dr. McCoy depends on drugs and instruments to effect healing. In this fictional tomorrow, a scan with an instrument can heal instantly. A diagnostic scanner has been reduced to a hand-held model.

The episode entitled *The Immunity Syndrome* is a clever take on viruses invading an organism. In this case it is a single-celled, 11,000-mile-long virus invading the galaxy. The *Enterprise* acts as an antibody and destroys it before it can reproduce. This is typical of current approaches to healing. There is nothing new here—just a clever view of a larger model.

Current *natural* approaches to healing belie the vision of *Star Trek* except for one episode. In it we probably see a closer version of what our future healing techniques will be than in any other dramatic offering. We saw it also in the way Jesus did it.

Healing Touch

Here we have the story about "Gem" in the episode called *The Empath*, where we not only get a glimpse of the future but a review of the past as well. We have all heard of faith healing, and who is there who does not know that Jesus healed the sick with a glance? He told us we could do the same—and more.

In this episode, Kirk, Spock, and McCoy are picking up two men on an outpost in the Minarvan system, where an approaching nova is being monitored. But the two men who should have been there are gone, and tapes of their last minutes on the outpost show they heard a piercing sound and then disappeared. Soon they also hear the sound and disappear. They end up underground on the same planet, where they discover the two men they were to pick up being preserved, but dead, in large specimen tubes. Two aliens, Lal and Thann, are engaged in torturing people they capture to test an empath from a neighboring planet, the only other character there. They can rescue only one planet's population from the nova, but there are two that need rescuing, so they are trying to find out which is more worthy.

"Gem," which is a name McCoy gives her to avoid calling her "Hey you!" is mute, having no vocal chords—a feature of her species—so we see her part played in mime. She is so sensitive to the pain of others that she takes their injuries upon herself, which heals them, and then she heals herself. When Dr. McCoy's injuries from torture are so severe they are life threatening, she hesitates to take them on herself. But she succumbs to her compassion and tries. This is an example of what we mean when we say that love heals. When we love others so much that we are willing to take on their pain, then we are potential healers.

Kirk points out to the aliens responsible for all this that their *own* empathy is lacking, since they callously torture and almost kill others to find out what they want to know. Recognizing that he is right, they take Gem with them and let the *Enterprise* officers go.

Some of the flamboyant evangelical faith healers we watch on television and other places may be frauds, whereas others could be genuine. However, I am one who has to experience something myself before believing it.

I was attending classes in New York in the early Seventies,

95

and in one class I had a severe headache. Since I kept rubbing my head, the teacher asked if I had a headache, and when I said I did, he put one of his hands on the nape of my neck and the other on my forehead for only a minute or so. My headache disappeared, and he commented, "That *is* a bad one!" When I asked how he knew, he said he had taken it on himself, but that it would be gone from him in a few minutes, and evidently it was.

Many extremely empathetic and compassionate people can do this and do not even know it. Some experience it as feeling the pain of others when they are around sick people. They may really believe they have an illness, but when examined there is nothing organically wrong. As a reflex we are tempted to accuse them of being hypochondriacs, but in some cases they have just unconsciously taken on the pain of someone they have passed on the street. Without training, they don't know what to do with it or even where it came from.

Spiritual Healing

Edgar Cayce, sometimes known as "the Sleeping Prophet," was the most documented psychic healer of recent times. He was able to go into a trance, and through astral travel visit those who wrote to him for help. He could diagnose their illnesses and give them instructions for healing without even seeing them in person. The instructions for these natural remedies are archived at the Association for Research and Enlightenment in Virginia Beach, Virginia, and have helped countless others long after his death. The evidence is too overwhelming to dismiss.

Reiki and other Asian healing techniques are also very effective. These are based on the idea that wellbeing comes from balanced or spiritually guided energy or life force. Reiki comes from two Japanese words: *Rei* ("God's wisdom" or "higher power") and *Ki* ("life force energy"). It does not negate the use of medicine or other aids to promote healing, but instead adds to their effectiveness by supplying additional healing energy. It is simple and safe, but also is enhanced when one lives from high ideals and virtue.

Above all, *love* is a healing energy. I often wonder if all sickness is just an absence of love, whether a lack of love for oneself or others. We know now that not only do married people live longer than singles, but babies thrive who have much more than their physical needs met. Robust youngsters are those who get positive attention and are the center of their parents' lives. So it is not a huge leap of faith to conclude that healing has, at its core, loving attention between people—the healer and the healed. Perhaps illness in all forms is a cry for help when one needs the care and attention of other people to feel connected.

A Course in Miracles says that illness is anger taken out on the body. Anger can be an emotion one feels if there is an absence of love in one's life. But it can also be anger directed at others. Louise Hay in her book *Heal Your Body* and Alice Steadman's *Who's the Matter with Me* have even broken down parts of the body that represent what we are angry about or what blockages we are creating to stop the flow of healthy energy in our bodies. Our bodies are intelligent right down to the cellular level and can reveal information about our psychological wellbeing through illness. Illness or "*dis*-ease" is a primary way the body lets us know about uneasiness of the spirit. It is a form of communication. One of the best ways to heal is not to take a handful of pills but to ask oneself *why* the body is trying to get your attention. Further, the other side of love is forgiveness. *A Course in Miracles* says that forgiveness is what this world needs more than anything else, and the basis of forgiveness is unconditional love. It is in the healing of the spirit that we heal the body.

In the Manual for Teachers, the third book of *A Course in Miracles*, it is also stated that to effect healing "...involves an understanding of what the illusion of sickness is for." It further states, "Healing is accomplished the instant the sufferer no longer sees any value in pain. Who would choose suffering unless he thought it brought him something, and something of value to him? He must think it is a small price to pay for something of greater worth. For sickness is an election; a decision." Those are harsh words for a suffering person to hear. No one who has a serious disease consciously believes it was a decision. It is, of course, an *unconscious* decision. Perhaps a person found that the greatest loving attention came from his or her parents when s/he was ill. So if one is feeling unloved or lonely, it can be a request for attention and love. "It worked before," the unconscious reasons, "so why not now?"

Prayer Heals 97

Prayer is more than just words. It is an affirmation that affects subatomic particles to form into stated reality. It is energy. There are many documented illustrations of healing prayer, but one that is from my own family involves my sister.

Barbara was 13 when she was hospitalized with rheumatic fever. She was so seriously ill she wasn't allowed to get out of bed without assistance. One day the family minister came to the hospital to visit, and he told her that she would be healed when she believed it. Being an impressionable, innocent child with no doubt that he knew what he was talking about, she believed him. She said to herself, "Now I'm healed so I can get out of bed by myself." She got up on her own and went to the bathroom. The nurses were frantic, and there was a commotion, but from that day on, she was healed.

PART THREE

Vision of the Future

CHAPTER NINE

Parallel Universes and Time Travel

I myself believe that there will one day be time travel, because when we find that something isn't forbidden by the over-arching laws of physics we usually eventually find a technological way of doing it.
~ David Deutsch

Speaking of the laws of physics, Murray Gell-Mann, the physicist who discovered and named the quark, went by a law he postulated himself. If the laws of physics do not specifically forbid something, he decided, then it *must* exist. (It was on this basis that he went quark-hunting in the first place, because physics didn't forbid the particle's existence.) Some people are brighter than the sun.

Some of the most fascinating possibilities in *Star Trek* dealt with the concept of time and the nature of the universe. If I had not had a little preparation from the *Star Trek* stories, I might not have even understood what Seth was trying to explain in *Seth Speaks* regarding the way we live our incarnations simultaneously. He explained that time is a construct of our own making and is non-existent outside our own earth script—at least not as we know it. It is our fourth dimension. This is not new. People were calling time the fourth dimension back in the 19th century. We are used to the ideas that Edgar Cayce outlined about reincarnation, but when Seth told us that we live those lives simultaneously, but in different time dimensions, it was a little mind-blowing.

It helps to understand that subatomic particles can exist as one indivisible particle but be in as many as 3,000 places at once. The movie *What the Bleep!? – Down the Rabbit Hole* is convincing in its explanation that we are in a holographic universe of our own creation through our personal choices. Since the brain processes billions of bits of information each minute, but we are aware of only about 2,000 of them, there is far more that we are *not* aware of than what we *are* aware of. Our "reality" is just our individual brains' limited interpretation of what is observed, depending on *which* 2,000 bits of information we are choosing to notice that minute. Other brains have different interpretations because they are making different choices. That is why two witnesses rarely see the same thing in an accident.

Twin or Parallel Universes

If subatomic particles can be *one and indivisible* at the same time that they can be in as many as 3,000 places at once, and if we are all made of subatomic particles, then it is possible to be living parallel lives at the same time and yet each of us remain part of one, indivisible soul. In fact, if we are *all one,* then *collectively* we could be living on another Earth in another galaxy in a parallel *collective* reality. In the quantum world there is a phenomenon called "entanglement," whereby two subatomic particles can be separated by an enormous amount of space—scientists say as far away as the other end of the galaxy—and when something affects one, it instantly affects the other. They are somehow connected, and time and space are not factors affecting them. I was reminded of this when Spock "felt" the deaths of 400 Vulcans when the USS *Intrepid* was destroyed in the episode, *The Immunity Syndrome.*

In *Bread and Circuses,* we are introduced to the idea of a duplicate Earth. In this Earth, though, Rome never fell. More than 2,000 years later, although the twin planet has progressed close to our level of technology, and even some clothing is the same, slavery and brutal games at the Colosseum are still flourishing. Also, there is a resistance group called the Worshippers of the Sun. These are bands of people who live in caves and would be persecuted by the government if they were found. They believe in love, non-violence, and brotherhood and are against the brutality of slavery. Later, the *Enterprise* officers discover that they misunderstood the meaning of "Sun" and that it was really the "Son," the Christ, whom the rebels were worshipping. Even Christian redemption was duplicated on this parallel or twin world.

The parallel universe theory was explored again in *The Tholian Web,* but instead of a duplicate world, the *Enterprise* enters an unexplored, unstable fabric of space where dimensional interphases occur. Their mission is to find a lost ship, the USS *Defiant,* which has been missing for three weeks. When they come

101

upon it, all aboard are not only dead, they killed one another. It appears to have been a mutiny. Also, the ship is dissolving. McCoy discovers that the dead bodies and even metal objects are so ethereal he can put his hand through them. The ship is phasing out of one dimension into another.

This section of space is beginning to affect the *Enterprise*, as well. Energy is being drained, so only three of those who beamed over to the "ghost" ship in space suits can be brought back at one time. Gallant Captain Kirk sends his three officers back first, leaving him alone. They are unable to bring him back, and he disappears with the *Defiant* when it completely vanishes into another dimension. Spock explains that several universes co-exist in the same physical space but are invisible to one another except at specific times when they intersect. They are hoping to retrieve the captain when this happens—hopefully before his oxygen supply in the space suit runs out.

Meanwhile, the Tholians show up and demand that the *Enterprise* leave their region of space. Since the *Enterprise* crew must wait to retrieve the captain, they have to maintain their position. The Tholians, therefore, weave a force field around them. Meanwhile, various crew members see a ghostly form of the captain floating in space, so they have something to lock onto when they break free of the web. Captain Kirk is beamed aboard safely.

The idea of many dimensions is fascinating and has enthralled the inquisitive for a long time. We all know that time is relative—not only because of our perceptions of how it "drags on" or "flies by" and because of Einstein's relativity theory—but it could also be relative in various dimensions, if it exists at all outside our own three-dimensional plane. I always thought, for example, that if we lived in a two-dimensional world, it would take "time" to perceive a table, since we'd have to perceive it in sections—building one plane of it at a time, if we could even conceptualize the idea of a table in that kind of universe. We would not "see" it all in an instant as we can in a three-dimensional world. That made sense to me, except that I was still "constructing" a three-dimensional object!

102   It is hard to get out of our own three-dimensional concept. For years, I thought of a two-dimensional world as being similar to what I described above—that it *built* three dimensions *using* time. But in its purest form, a two-dimensional world would not be able to conceive of a table with height because height would not exist. In

1884 there was a short book published called *Flatland: A Romance of Many Dimensions* by Edwin A. Abbott. This book, which is still in print, describes life from a two-dimensional point of view and opens the imagination to the possibility of many dimensions. It is still as relevant today as it was over a century ago. The narrator, a resident of Flatland, explains his society, but he also introduces us to "Lineland" and "Spaceland," giving the reader an exercise in perceiving the limitations of each dimension. Reading such a book stretches the mind, so it is easier to understand the concept of more or less than three dimensions and, from what current superstring theory is showing us, "many more" is likely.

Dimensions and Time

When I first began studying astrology, it was hard for me to grasp the idea that future probabilities, in a narrow range of possibilities, could be foretold and described. The proof of it was in being able to do it using hindsight without knowing what had actually occurred. However, since it was in the past, it was easily verified when we were able to describe what happened energetically in that past time. In class we learned the mathematical techniques necessary to review a person's life and conclude what had happened to that person in the past— not events, necessarily, but emotional crises or turning points. By doing that, since we could clearly see the mathematical correlations to past events in a person's life, it was not difficult to be convinced that it worked in assessing the future as well. I will never forget one skeptical client's remark when I reviewed his first 54 years. He said, "When you were not right on the money, you were knockin' at the door." If this art/science works so well, then there has to be a further dimension beyond time. Now we're finding out, through forays into string theory, that there are possibly as many as ten dimensions, one of which is time.

I don't remember which of my teachers described it, but one asked the class to imagine being an observer of a "belt of time" moving slowing along in a particular rhythm, which would be the measurement of time increments as we know them—that is weeks, months, years, and so forth—with dramas being enacted on the belt at designated points of time. If one could rise above the belt and look down, one could see what was coming and what went before. That may be a simplistic way of explaining the concept, but with the idea that time is relative to what can be perceived all at once simultaneously, it made more sense to

103

me. It was especially clear when I was able to see planetary cycles synchronizing with actual events as they occurred in hundreds of lives over the ensuing years, as I did this professionally and observed my clients' unfolding dramas. (We are not talking about newspaper column astrology here, but *real* astrology, which is at least a couple of dimensions more sophisticated.)

In the book, *Flatland,* the author explains that when one is imbedded in Flatland, shapes cannot be discerned because one would have to be able to rise *above* the shapes to be able to see them, and since height does not exist there, everything *to them* appears to be a line, a curve, an angle, or a point. In their society they have learned how to tell if an entity is a square, triangle, line, or whatever, but anything involving height is impossible for them to comprehend. That is how I think the dimension of time is. We can only comprehend it within the confines of a three-dimensional mentality. I would never have been able to grasp this about time had I not studied astrology and observed firsthand how we can "read" the past and the future—at least read the probabilities. Since quantum mechanics tells us how particles show multiple possibilities until a choice has been made, the future is always potential, but the timing is not all that arbitrary. Perhaps one with access to a fifth-dimensional mentality could *see* that actual "belt of time" moving along with potential event choices unfolding in pre-determined order.

Many of the *Star Trek* episodes concerned time travel, and one that we could all relate to was *Tomorrow Is Yesterday,* since the time trip went to the mid-Sixties, when this first aired. The *Enterprise* is accidentally thrown back into the mid-20th century just before the first manned moon launch. It was our own contemporary time, so we could well appreciate the adventure concerning the inadvertent capture of the pilot who is taken aboard to save his life. The *Enterprise* puts his aircraft in a tractor beam, which is too much for it to sustain. As it is breaking up, the pilot has to be rescued. In some ways it is amusing to compare the two time periods, but the sobering difficulty lies in how history might change if anyone has a glimpse into the future. It occurs to the crew that if this pilot were allowed to take information about this future time home with him, then their own lives might not even exist in the future affected by that change. There is the quandary of *choice* again.

There was a television drama years ago about this topic. Some people going back in time were told to be very careful not

104

to touch or disturb anything because it could change the future. Someone killed a bug—just one annoying insect—and when he returned to his own time, there was a different language and a totally different culture. He had no one to go home to—all because he had killed a bug.

Time Travel as Solution and Punishment

The City on the Edge of Forever and *Assignment: Earth* are two other episodes that dealt with the return to 20th-century America and avoiding interference with history, but our imaginations really got a treat with *All Our Yesterdays*.

The planet Sarpeidon is about to be annihilated, as its sun, becoming a nova, will expand to extinguish it. Spock, Kirk, and McCoy beam down and are surprised to find themselves in a huge library with a librarian, Mr. Atoz, who urges them to quickly look at past periods of the planet. Confused, they try to comply, but while Kirk is observing a past that resembles 17th-century England, he hears a woman screaming and rushes toward the sound to help. He inadvertently is thrown back to the time he had been observing in the library's viewer. McCoy had been looking at a scene from the planet's ice age, and when he and Spock try to follow Kirk, they are thrown into the same forbidding and icy environment they had just been observing.

The problem occurs when they all realize they needed to be "prepared" by the librarian, using a machine called the Atavachron, which alters the time traveler to be able to physically adapt to the new time he would supposedly live in the rest of his life, to escape the nova. Once prepared, there is no returning to the previous time. But if not prepared, one cannot remain long in the past or death is inevitable.

This planet had two uses for the Atavachron machine. One, it allowed people to live in any time period they wished as a solution for the end of their planet's existence, and two, it was used as punishment to sentence undesirable people to live out their lives in harsh conditions. Such was the case with Zarabeth, the lovely woman whom Spock and McCoy discover in the ice age they enter. She finds them freezing and leads them to a cave warmed by a subterranean hot spring. Spock is reverting to his 105 primitive roots since it is theoretically 5,000 years earlier, when Vulcans were still savages. He is attracted to Zarabeth and would gladly remain in this ice age with her. But later they discover that McCoy cannot go back unless he and Spock return through the portal together, just as they had gone into it, and McCoy does not want to stay.

Meanwhile, Kirk is arrested as a thief because he helped the screaming woman, who is a thief herself. He is considered an accomplice. Also, he heard McCoy's voice through the portal, so he is accused of witchcraft, since he was talking to "spirits." He discovers that a magistrate who is in charge of his arrest is actually one of the citizens escaping the nova, and this man shows him where the portal is, with instructions about returning. All return safely and in time for the librarian to leave for his designated time period and to escape the nova themselves.

We are fascinated by the idea of traveling through time, as a whole variety of TV shows and movies on the subject give witness. Is it possible? Well, if time is really a dimension and doesn't exist outside our three-dimensional world, as we understand it, then why not? Other things on *Star Trek* are materializing. Just today there was an article on the Internet about a garment embedded with sensors that creates audible music while one plays an air guitar when wearing it. That is one step toward the garment that Miranda wore in *Is There in Truth No Beauty?* with its web of sensors that allowed her to "see." There was also news recently about success in transporting matter, similar to the transporter on the *Enterprise*. We would have scoffed a few years ago at such a thing being possible, but we are witnessing the miracles of *Star Trek* appearing one after another as the years progress.

The laws of physics have been shaken up since discovering the maverick world of particle physics. Things that do not seem possible actually happen, causing scientists to scratch their heads in bewilderment. Physicist Richard Feynman found that some electrons can travel backward (or forward) in time, but when they travel backward they looked like their antiparticle, called the positron. Remember that all matter is ultimately built on particles. Particles form atoms, and atoms form molecules. The universe is made of them, so if particles can in some way travel backward through time, this fact will spark the imagination of someone to make it a reality on a larger scale.

We are now at the cutting edge of using quantum mechanics in computers, which will probably make electronics obsolete. Once quantum computers are commonplace, who knows what we may do?

Time Travel and Reincarnation

In *Seth Speaks*, the best-selling chronicles of Jane Robert's channeling of *Seth*, a spirit whose words are recorded there, Seth says that our greater selves cannot exist in only three dimensions and that *parts* of itself manifest, or project, in time and space. Further, since time does not exist outside our experience the way we perceive it here, we are also living all our incarnations at once—simultaneously in different dimensions. He tells us that we visit other lifetimes in our dreams. When first confronted with this kind of "other dimension" information, it can seem daunting and hard to believe, but for some reason we understand best after we can see something dramatized.

Not too long ago I saw a movie, part of the *Spiritual Cinema Circle's* offerings, called *An Angel for May* (also available for sale on the internet) which helped to clarify the ideas from the Seth material. There seem to be many movies in this genre lately. In this one, not only was there a time travel component, but the past was altered by the present time's participant in the "past" incident. Since he could go to the past at will and participate in lives going on in World War II, then come back and see the same characters—but 60 years older, it all seemed to be happening simultaneously. Why is it that we don't experience this if, in fact, it's possible? There may be two reasons. First from Seth, on page 317 of *Seth Speaks*:

Western man has chosen to focus his energy outward and largely ignore inner realities. The social and cultural aspects, and even the religious ones, automatically inhibit such experiences from childhood on. There is no social benefit at all connected with projections in your society, and many taboos against it.

Second, Mike Dooley, in his series *Infinite Possibilities*, points out that we are in a collective "agreement" about our reality. Until the scales are tipped to the side where more than a few are having experiences that are out of the ordinary, skepticism will prevail, and our unawareness of these realities will continue. As soon as many are reporting unusual experiences, then there will be a shift in consciousness, and we all will then form a new agreement 107 about what is real and what is not. It took a century, from the time Galileo first espoused the fact, for mankind to accept that the sun was the center of our planetary system. Now we cannot imagine how anyone could have thought otherwise. The unusual behavior of quantum physics is leading us to another major shift in perception, which will alter our beliefs permanently. *Star Trek*, however, as well as *A Course in Miracles*, have prepared us for this new shift well in advance. All that shallower people will say about it, probably, is that the "way out" things on *Star Trek* are coming true. It matters not, so long as we grow collectively into a more advanced spiritual state.

CHAPTER TEN

Duality and Parallel Universes

The goal is non-dualistic – as long as there is a "knower"
and "known" you are in dualism.
~ Baba Ram Dass

Modern psychology has familiarized us with the concept of
split personalities, light and dark sides of consciousness, and even
multiple personalities inhabiting one body. This is graphically
dramatized several times in the series. In each case, the darker or
"shadow" side of the psyche is portrayed as irrational, bordering
on the insane, with evil intent. This is the war between good and
evil, residing in us because of original sin, according to Christian
doctrine. There is a similar, though less moralistic, message
in *A Course in Miracles*, wherein the ego is described often as
"insane." We have this "enemy within" that constantly tries to
run our lives by tempting us to be deceptive, jealous, controlling,
or a myriad of other unsavory emotions. Even as it seduces us
with the temptation to feel "special" or "unfairly treated," there
is another, more rational side (often portrayed as an angelic
conscience sitting on our shoulder) reminding us it is not true.
This is a duality we all feel.

Sometimes, though, the duality is a good one, and then
it is just a matter of keeping the two energies in balance or in
their best ratio. Both are needed. These energies are referred
to by some as the *yin* and *yang* (receptive and active) aspects of
personality, while others call it the *anima* and *animus* sides of our
nature—our female and male polarities.

The Enemy Within is a particularly interesting presentation
of the roles of duality, showing how necessary the *yin* and *yang*
factors are.

While gathering specimens on Alpha 177, Technician Fisher
cuts himself and has to beam up to the *Enterprise*. But there is

difficulty in doing so. Later, when the captain comes back on board, he seems weak and unsteady as he steps off the transporter. Scott exits the transporter room with the captain, leaving it unattended, and while he is gone, a duplicate of Captain Kirk beams aboard, leaves the room, and roams freely around the ship. Later, when Scott returns, he beams aboard an animal that Sulu has befriended and seconds later observes a second animal beaming aboard that appears to be a replica. However, because the first animal is docile and the second one ferocious, Scott mentions that it is not the same but an *opposite* of the first version.

Meanwhile, two dramas unfold. First, we discover that the two Kirks are also opposite. The first one is docile and indecisive while the second is aggressive, cunning, and irrational. When the second one tries to rape Yeoman Janice Rand, she scratches his face, giving others a mark by which they can identify him. Second, the remaining landing party cannot be beamed aboard because they fear the same split in personalities will happen with them. However, they are freezing in sub-zero temperatures as night falls on this planet.

The evil side of Kirk is determined to take over the ship and after applying make-up over his scratches, he obtains a phaser. The mild side meanwhile is losing command and cannot make a decision. When they finally encounter each other, Spock easily recognizes the more aggressive and dangerous side and uses his neck pinch to send him into unconsciousness.

Although Spock is fascinated with this phenomenon and would like to study the two halves of Kirk, time is of the essence to save the members of the landing party, who are by now almost frozen to death. After experimenting unsuccessfully with the animal that was "split," they transport the two Kirks together back to the planet, in hopes that the two parts will be reintegrated. It works, and Kirk and the landing party are rescued just in time. They conclude, somewhat obviously, that the more aggressive side of the personality has a purpose, and that it is necessary in roles of leadership.

Other episodes relying on this theme are *The Naked Time*, *Mirror, Mirror*, and *The Alternative Factor*. In *The Naked Time* the crew is infected by some kind of fluid that brings out their less-inhibited selves—like being drunk. But, in *Mirror, Mirror* and *The Alternative Factor*, there is a dual theme. These two episodes combine parallel universes *and* duality. Granted, parallel universes are a *kind* of

110

duality, but they do not have to be restricted to only two. There could be many. Further, they do not have to be versions of the positive and negative sides of personalities, as portrayed in other episodes. But first a bit of background.

Alternative Parallel Universes

Robert Monroe, in his book *Journeys Out of the Body*, describes his discovery of what appears to be a parallel universe. In this fascinating account of his experiences with astral travel, he says that when he leaves his body in a particular way, it takes him to a place that is strange to him. Vehicles are designed differently, as well as clothing and other material things, but he "knows" he is a particular man in this place. He finds the man and visits his life from time to time. However, this alternative version of himself is not an opposite in temperament. He is simply another part of his over soul or greater self.

At one time Monroe experimentally inhabited his alter ego's body and was surprised to find he didn't gain access to the other man's thoughts, knowledge, skills, or memories. He retained his own. This shows that our minds are not our brains, if one believes Robert Monroe's account (and there is no reason why we shouldn't). When he left his body on his many astral excursions, he took his "mind" with him and was unaware of the body left behind on his bed. Mr. Monroe's book reveals a great deal about life outside our physical selves, but over and over the main issue is that consciousness does *not* reside in our bodies or brains, but rather in another part of us that is invisible (at our current state of development) and does not rely on the body for existence at all. In fact, the body is something of an encumbrance, no doubt needed for our "earth school" experience, but not really part of our essential consciousness.

Seth, in *Seth Speaks*, calls these parallel experiences different "streams of consciousness" and explains that there is a deep river of this consciousness in each *over soul.* But we pay attention to just a small part of it, ignoring other experiences our greater self is experiencing simultaneously. We are not aware of them because we are focused on just one tiny drama of our over soul's total awareness. It seems similar to the idea that a subatomic particle can be in 3,000 places at once but collapses into one state when we "focus on" or "choose" one. At the moment of choice, the other probabilities disappear. Apparently, though, the over soul would rather keep all of its "probable selves" in play, perhaps to

111

learn much more than it would if it chose just one of its "selves." Seth says, "*These other streams of consciousness, however, are connected with other self-forms that you do not perceive. The body, in other words, is simply one manifestation of what you are in one reality, but in these other realities you have other forms.*"

Mirror, Mirror is an episode that explores good and evil polarities—all as a result of choice—of entities in parallel universes. Some of the officers of the *Enterprise* accidentally trade places with their counterparts in a parallel universe where the Federation has developed more barbarically—in fact, similarly to the Klingons.

In *The Alternative Factor*, there are two men, each called Lazarus, who are exact counterparts from two different universes—one matter and the other anti-matter. If they were to meet fact to face, it would be cataclysmic. The resultant explosion would destroy the known universe, according to the script. Interestingly, these two are presented as mental opposites—one sane and rational, the other a raving madman. The mad Lazarus is sure that the sane Lazarus is his enemy and is frantic to destroy him. The sane one knows what is going on and is trying to trap his insane counterpart in a corridor between the two dimensions so that a disaster can be averted, which he succeeds in doing in the end.

Another version of this idea is expressed in the previously mentioned book, Richard Bach's *One*. He explores the idea that whenever we make a choice, we split into two realities, each living the outcome of the choice made and (theoretically) not made. From that point on, none of the cast members of the play know about the others. In Mr. Bach's book, he is able to visit other versions of life choices for himself and his wife. We see what would have happened if one choice had been made over another. This concept is a bit hard to imagine, but I suppose, if true, then when we unite with all our alternative selves eventually, we will have learned much more this way.

CHAPTER ELEVEN

Androids and Artificial Intelligence

Some people worry that artificial intelligence will make us feel inferior, but then, anybody in his right mind should have an inferiority complex every time he looks at a flower.
~ Alan C. Kay

When we think of what would happen if we lost all that is on our computers, we become anxious and virtually seize up at the thought. It would be a disaster. Dependency on artificial intelligence has crept into our culture, from our daily PC use to verbal directions computerized in our cars. Everyday use of androids is a mere breath away, and in fact, prototypes are already developed. Japan demonstrated an extremely life-like lady within the last year. Before yellow-eyed Data came along in the second *Star Trek* series, the original series had several examples of androids that deceived our intrepid officers of the *Enterprise*.

In the episode *What Are Little Girls Made Of?*, the *Enterprise* is orbiting planet Exo III to discover what has become of Dr. Roger Korby, Nurse Christine Chapel's fiancé. When they find him, he insists that only Kirk and Christine join him in underground caverns he has discovered. We learn he has also discovered an ancient civilization's machines and methods for creating androids. In fact, we are surprised, later in the drama, that Korby himself is an android, as are his assistants. Before his organic body died, he implanted his memory and personality into an identical android "body." It guarantees immortality.

Korby wants to leave the planet to seed the universe with androids, and to do this he duplicates Kirk so that he can take over the *Enterprise* for his own use. But while going through the process of cloning, Kirk plants false and misleading thoughts into his android duplicate, which later alerts Spock to which one is the real Kirk.

113

Just as Data in the *Star Trek TNG* series struggled with emotion, which eluded him, these androids have the same problem. Even though the contents of the brain have been retrieved from a human subject, they are simply stored data with no emotional content.

Our first explanation is that they have no soul. Since they are machines, they could not possibly have the capacity for love, fear, depression, et al. Two things are highlighted in this episode—one, that the androids followed directions to the letter, as when Ruk is ordered not to harm Nurse Chapel under any circumstances, and two, that androids cannot feel conscience or love. Therefore, there is no real freedom of choice and no ability to feel on an emotional level.

Common sense tells us that we are more than machines. Our contradictory behavior, which begins at birth, speaks of a complex, multi-dimensional emotional life that transcends machinery. Seth, in *Seth Speaks,* tells us the soul is much more creative and complex than our religions grant it, and that our concept of a "soul" is limited, actually, by our three-dimensional concepts.

One such concept is that of "soul mates." We see ourselves as either male or female, when, in fact, the soul is androgynous. We can manifest as one or the other, but not both. Elisabeth Haich explained it beautifully in her book, *Initiation,* when she compared it to opposites. One cannot have light in a room and have it remain in darkness at the same time. So one's soul cannot manifest as both male and female at the same time. The term "soul mate" is merely the other half of *yourself,* which you unconsciously hunger for but cannot possibly find in this lifetime, since both cannot manifest physically together. Those of you who may feel you have found your soul mate, rest assured that this is only a close proximity. Usually, as Carl Jung postulates, we consider our soul mate to be the embodiment of the inner ideal of the anima, if a man—or animus, if a woman.

More than all that, though, our souls have inexplicable experiences, such as "gut feelings" that later turn out to be true. We have intuition, whereby we sense things without concrete evidence. Our capacity for compassion and sacrifice, as well as self-preservation, bespeaks a depth of emotion that would be impossible to duplicate in a machine. If it is true that each of us is only a small expression of a greater *over soul,* then the significance of the soul's power and purpose grows exponentially. In fact, how would a scientist program a robot or an android to *dream,* which is another function of the soul?

The question is, "Can we duplicate a soul?" Also, "Where does the soul come from?" And ultimately, "What *is* a soul?" Some may call it consciousness—that is, an energy conscious of itself. If we are only our minds, that is, an accumulation of knowledge, then where does creative imagination come from? Who is thinking the thoughts? Actually, as long as we are in the three-dimensional arena we have chosen, we may never know the origin of the soul, its expansiveness, nor exactly what it *is*—since we are limited by our three-dimensional viewpoint, much as the residents of Flatland could not conceive of the dimension of height. And we certainly cannot duplicate what we cannot define or understand.

But That Doesn't Stop Us from Trying!

In *Requiem for Methuselah* we see a genius pushing the boundaries of possibility. We are told in the Bible how Methuselah lived to be 969 years old. The main character in this story, Flint, is thousands of years old and has *been* Brahms and Michelangelo. Original works abound in his residence on the planet Holberg 917-G, where he has gone to escape but also found his mortality. Since he left the atmosphere of Earth, the source of his longevity, he discovered he was no longer immortal. The *Enterprise* landing party, thinking the planet uninhabited, have beamed down to find an antidote to Rigellian fever, which has stricken the crew. They encounter Flint, with his servant robot and his ward, Rayna Kapec, who is really an android of the perfect woman Flint has created for himself.

Flint recognizes immediately that Kirk and Rayna are attracted to each other; therefore, he arranges for them to have time together so that Kirk can bring out dormant (in Flint's opinion) emotional feelings in Rayna. The servant robot is sent to gather and process the antidote to Rigellian fever, Ryetalyn, allowing time for the visitors to look around and get to know Rayna and Flint.

Our credulousness is really challenged when Kirk becomes so emotionally intense so soon—it seems too much, and for only superficial reasons. Even after he discovers many prior prototypes of Rayna, revealing that she is an android, Kirk continues to be infatuated. Flint is in love with his creation of the "perfect woman," who obviously also matches Kirk's anima, and Flint

115

wants her to return his love. He believes that Kirk can awaken this emotion in her android body. When it appears that Kirk is successful in igniting passion in Rayna, her circuitry fails, and she "dies."

Alas, it *is* fiction after all. Many other shows, such as *The Twilight Zone*, have explored this topic. Nothing really new here, but a discussion of *Star Trek* would not be complete if it was not mentioned. And it points out that our dreams of creating androids ignore not only the gender aspect that hasn't incarnated (the soul mate), but also the many hundreds of parallel lives that the over soul has going, if Seth is right.

What About the Reverse?

So it is apparent, as far as we know, that an android cannot be built that possesses its own soul, as we understand it. In the episode *Return to Tomorrow*, we have an interesting twist on this theme, in which there are entities seeking to house their own souls in an android body. They call them their minds instead of souls, but from their behavior, which includes choices based on ethics, passion, and love, we have to conclude that there is more preserved than just their minds. Since souls inhabit a body, it is not so far-fetched that souls could possess and occupy an android body. After all, Robert Monroe discovered in his *Journeys out of the Body* that his consciousness was not dependent on his body. We do know that someone else's soul can possess a body—so why not an android?

The *Enterprise* answers a distress call from the planet Arret, which is believed to be dead. There they find a subterranean chamber where there are globes containing the disembodied spirits of three people—the planet's former leader, his wife, and another man.

Star Trek's names are intriguing. One *Star Trek* website says that Arret is Terra spelled backward and is located in about the same place as Earth (Terra) in the negative universe. However, it is also French for "stop" and the basis for the word, "arrest" which, of course, brings something to a stop. The disembodied souls in this story are stopped on their planet from leaving or doing anything. They are encased in globes, and if the globes are destroyed, so are they (though this is contradicted later).

Their individual names are also suitable. The leader is named Sargon. It is from the Akkadian "Sarukinu" meaning "the true king." There was a historical figure of this name beginning

116

his reign around 2334 BC. He was a castaway baby, according to legend, taken out of the Euphrates by a gardener who raised him. He eventually founded and reigned over the Assyrian Empire for 56 years. It resembles the story of Moses but pre-dates it by a thousand years. *Star Trek*'s Sargon, however, seems to be much more compassionate and ethical than the historical one.

Sargon's wife, Thalassa, is named for the Greek personification of the Mediterranean Sea, or perhaps after one of Neptune's moons. One of the name's descriptions is "a vast, lonely sea on abandoned shores." It is very descriptive of a lost soul looking for union with her husband.

And the third person, a man named Henoch, is named for a son of the biblical Cain. Another patriarch was given this name and was the father of Methuselah, but it is probably the former the writers had in mind, since Henoch turns out to be a traitor and murderer in this story.

In this drama, Sargon and his wife want to occupy Kirk and Dr. Anne Mulhall's bodies long enough to build androids to house their consciousnesses—instead of the globes—so they will be able to live fulfilling lives. Henoch occupies Spock's body supposedly for the same purpose. They succeed in transporting their souls into the three bodies from the *Enterprise*, temporarily housing their hosts' consciousnesses in the globes, but Henoch has no intention of returning Spock's body and intends to kill Sargon so that he can have Thalassa. Henoch also has power over people's minds, so he controls the mind of Nurse Chapel to poison Sargon while Sargon occupies Kirk's body, thereby disposing of both leaders. He also destroys the globe containing Spock's consciousness, but Sargon had already transferred Spock's essence into Nurse Chapel, so he was not destroyed. Nurse Chapel defies the order to poison Kirk and injects Henoch instead, forcing him to leave Spock's body, at which time he is destroyed, supposedly because he has no globe to return to. In the end, Sargon and Thalassa are happy to leave physical existence behind and roam the universe disembodied. (The contradiction of their needing a vessel or container to survive seems to have been overlooked.)

One question that arises from this is whether the physical body interacts with the soul in some way to assist its function. It appears, from the writings of Robert Monroe, that this is not so. When he left his body in his book, *Journey's Out of the Body*, he "saw" with his non-corporeal eyes. He was unaware of his physical

117

body at all, which leaves us to conclude that something else—controlling sight, sensation, and experience is really in charge, using the body as a tool. The only time Monroe was aware of his body was when it "tugged" at him because of discomfort or danger of some sort. It was only when he re-entered his body that he would realize what it was that caused the tug.

It's All in the Programming

In the episodes *The Changeling; I, Mudd;* and *The Ultimate Computer,* the computers and androids destroy themselves. There are other storylines where this is the ultimate end, but in these it is the theme to use their programming against them for their own destruction.

In *The Changeling,* there is a fascinating tale of a collision when two computers on space probes had an accident, and a powerful and aggressive little probe sent out in 2020, named Nomad, acquired new programming from the probe with which it collided, to combine with his own original purpose. Through a mind meld with Nomad, Spock discovers that the original intent was to find new life forms. Nomad collided with "Tan-Ru," a unit programmed to sterilize soil samples from planets. The hybrid programming now believes the mission is to find life and sterilize imperfections. It believes that Kirk is its creator, since his name is similar to its inventor, Jackson Roykirk. So Kirk uses this mistake and a couple others to convince the computer that it, too, is imperfect and must self-destruct. It does, following its programming perfectly. No fear here.

Harcourt Fenton Mudd, in *I, Mudd,* is the center of attention as he takes over a planet populated by androids. The androids, however, learn about greed and deception through him, and their ultimate intention is to leave Mudd behind, with all the crew of the *Enterprise,* when the androids leave the planet on board the *Enterprise.* This is a funny episode where the androids are disabled and their plans foiled by a simple trick in logic. The lead android, Norman, through which the others function, is told that everything Mudd says is a lie. Then Mudd says, "I'm lying." The ensuing confusion blows Norman's circuits.

118

The Ultimate Computer is more sinister. Dr. Richard Daystrom, in an effort to prove himself, has invented a computer called the M-5, which will make any human captain of a starship redundant. It is installed on the *Enterprise* for testing in war games. At first, it performs admirably, but it is also gradually taking over the whole ship and draining more and more energy. Under query, it emerges that Dr. Daystrom programmed the M-5 with human engrams—his own. As M-5 gains in power, it shields itself from any interference from anyone, and so no one can prevent it from destroying an entire starship participating in war games. The fleet in the games assumes it is Kirk who is at fault, and Star Fleet grants them permission to destroy the *Enterprise* to stop it from annihilating any other ships. Kirk, to restore control of the ship, convinces the M-5 that it has *committed murder*, which is deeply against Daystrom's principles. So, out of conscience and guilt supplied by the human engrams, M-5 concludes it must kill itself as punishment. It lowers the ship's shields as the other ships are about to attack. The crew then shuts down the M-5 and the *Enterprise* plays dead. Kirk hopes that the other commanders recognize his hand in this ploy, and they do. The *Enterprise* is spared.

There is deep appreciation that when one programs a computer with human characteristics taken from a personality, *all* the personality—with flaws—will be present. More than that, though, is the ultimate truth that what we know of one another from experience, and what we feel intuitively, has greater value than any computer.

The True Ultimate Computer

The human brain is the most complex and mighty computer in existence (unless there are others we don't know about yet, such as alien brains). It is the human brain that *creates* artificial intelligence and ultimately controls it. Long before it was an issue, *Star Trek* offered a glimpse of what could happen *if* it got out of control or was used for the wrong purpose. Plenty of that is going on now with identity theft, war machines that defy the imagination, and invasion of privacy like we have never seen. Conversely, miracles are happening with computers that can scan and detect health issues, including instruments that allow surgery with minimum invasion. All depends on how they are used.

CHAPTER TWELVE

What Is Reality?

Reality is merely an illusion, although a very persistent one.
~ Albert Einstein

Early in the series, when we were introduced to *Mudd's Women*, there was a reference to our being what we believed ourselves to be. The placebo given to the women in place of the Venus drug worked as well as the real thing, because they *believed* it was what they were ingesting. We have been taught about this by motivational coaches, speakers, and psychologists. We know from experience that some people attract more success than others because they do not *expect* rejection or failure. They imagine success. Good results and success just gravitate to them. They are not necessarily better looking, smarter, or luckier. They just have a positive, expectant mental attitude. The opposite is also true. Those who give much energy to negative, fearful thinking attract negative and fearful situations.

What is not understood by many is that this is not merely wishful thinking. It is a metaphysical law, which is, in fact, based on laws of physics. These laws may not be fully understood yet, but research is pointing to possibilities of reality being as incredible as demonstrated in *Star Trek*. In a recent book called *The Field* by Lynne McTaggart, she reports on scientific experiments regarding the effect of mind and emotion on the vast subatomic particle field that permeates everything. These experiments reveal that we are much more in control of our lives than we may believe, and in fact, create our reality from moment to moment, depending upon how much attention and emotion we give to our thoughts and their content. In the *Star Trek* series, however, it goes beyond just manifesting reality for ourselves. There were creatures that could read minds, extract memories, and manifest them *for* their subjects!

Memory Becomes Reality

It is amazing that the pilot episode, *The Cage,* concerns this very subject, since in the mid-20th century we were just beginning to understand the mind-reality connection. The pilot itself was not aired as part of the original series but was presented later as a two-part episode called *The Menagerie,* which wove it into its drama.

On Stardate 3012.4, the *Enterprise* is taken to Starbase 6 because of an unexpected request supposedly initiated by former *Enterprise* captain, Christopher Pike, who has been severely injured. He is in a Space Age equivalent of a wheelchair, is badly burned and scarred, and cannot speak. Since he can only control lights that blink for "yes" and "no," no one can understand how he sent for the *Enterprise.* Actually, Spock had been on his crew long before, when they had an experience together on Talos IV, and at this time Spock is attempting to get Pike back to that planet, although there is a death penalty for anyone who goes there. Spock literally abducts the former Captain Pike and the *Enterprise* itself. Kirk and Mendez, the Starbase commodore, overtake the *Enterprise* and proceed to have a court-martial hearing for Spock, who has locked in the course for Talos IV and refuses to alter it. During the hearing, Spock explains his mission by telling a story through the old clips from *The Cage,* which are explained as being transmissions from Talos IV.

The pilot episode is about Captain Pike, captain of the *Enterprise,* being taken to Talos IV by the inhabitants there who are small in body size but with gigantic heads, indicative of their amazing mental powers. They have a woman by the name of Vina, whom they have rescued and who needs a partner so the Talosians can breed a slave population. They have determined that Captain Pike would be the perfect mate for her. He is put into a cage with Vina, and when he appears disinterested, some scenarios from Pike's past are re-enacted, with Vina playing central roles, so he will eventually fall in love with her. These scenes are created by the Talosians being able to read his subconscious memories and then projecting the memories as real, putting him in the drama as though he is re-living the event. Eventually, Vina tells him that the Talosians are not able to read minds when they are consumed with rage, so he resorts to inducing rage to finally get the upper hand. The Talosians innocently did not know that earth people cannot tolerate captivity, no matter how pleasant, so they let him go. In the end, it is seen that illusion propagated by the Talosians

121

is everywhere, even hiding damage that the *Enterprise* had done to the planet in trying to get the captain back.

In *The Menagerie*, the essentially kind Talosians have heard of Pike's tragic accident and are offering him a life with Vina now, by way of using their incredible mental abilities. At the end, it is seen that even the court-martial hearing was just a diversion, since Commodore Mendez was also an illusion to keep the ship on course without interference.

This episode could have been used as an example of the misuse of power, but the Talosians are not intending misuse of their abilities. They are benevolent and not aware that what they are doing is harmful. It is an example of what we can evolve into in terms of mental abilities and also the use of them. Vina, for instance, was torn apart when she originally crashed on Talos IV, but they put her together as best they could and gave her the illusion of great beauty, just as they are about to give Captain Pike the illusion of health and take away the painful reality of his paralysis, burns, and muteness. It can be debated whether we would some day be able to actually reconstruct whatever we like if the mind and emotions control subatomic particles, which are the building blocks of all reality. But the example here of the potential use of illusion is powerful.

An episode resembling this is *Spectre of the Gun*. The *Enterprise* encounters a warning buoy marking the territory of the Melkots. They are told to turn back but ignore the warning in the hope of gaining an alliance with them. When they transport to the planet's surface, a Melkotian informs them they will be punished, using Kirk's history as a model. A fragmentary replica, all that Kirk's memory holds of the town of Tombstone in the Old West of the late 19th century, manifests and the landing party slowly realizes they are going to re-enact the gunfight at the OK Corral between the Clanton gang and the Earps. Everyone they meet sees them as the Clanton gang. Since the Clantons were the losers in the shoot-out, and the group believes history cannot be changed, they assume they are doomed to die at five o'clock that day.

When the time comes, they are suddenly transported to a replica of the OK Corral where they face the Earps. By this time Spock has sufficient evidence that all is an illusion drawn from Kirk's memories. The main reason for his conclusion is that Chekov, as Billy Clanton, is killed prior to the gunfight, which did not happen historically. He surmises that if they all truly believe this is an illusion, and therefore not real, it simply cannot continue. To effect this conviction, he gives everyone in the party a mind meld that transfers his thoughts to theirs. As a result, the bullets from the Earps' guns rip harmlessly through them, and the drama is terminated.

This episode is one of the best at conveying what *A Course in Miracles* teaches, which is that anything that can be destroyed, including the body, is an illusion and therefore, not able to affect our core spirit, which cannot be destroyed. It is our true reality. Once we wake up and realize this, nothing has an effect on us, and we are able to create our reality as we wish. We see this in *The Matrix* when the hero realizes that all of the perceived life he is in is a computer simulation. He can then stop bullets in mid-air and they fall to the ground. This theme is repeated throughout the Course. Even our existence here is an illusion of our own creation. We ask for and create everything in our lives by the way we perceive what is real for us and what isn't. Some people cannot imagine or relate to poverty and so are never without funds. Others cannot relate to illness, and are therefore never sick. What we dwell upon, or fear will happen, becomes our reality. The Course teaches that there are only two realities, love and fear. We draw to us what we believe in most. If we believe in being fearful, then we attract more to fear. We have famous quotes that drive this crucial point home: "The only thing we have to fear is fear itself." (Franklin D. Roosevelt.) "That which I feared most has come upon me." (Job in the *Book of Job*.)

But if we believe in love, abundance, joy, and beauty, we will attract it all in whatever measure we *believe* we can have. Happiness is definitely an inside job.

Thoughts Create Reality

Illusion versus reality is a theme raised often in *Star Trek*, and the time was ripe for it. Motivational speakers were just beginning to appear with the message that we can achieve what we believe. *A Course in Miracles* was being scribed in the mid-Sixties with a similar message—that what we see around us is what we *expect*, and it has all been created by our own minds and choices. This is a great truth that could change everyday reality for anyone. *Star Trek* has played a huge role in familiarizing us with this concept. In fact, one episode brings home the fact that we must be careful what we wish for.

In *Shore Leave*, Captain Kirk decides to give the crew a break on a beautiful, Earth-like planet. But trouble brews when the

123

scouting party has some weird experiences. Dr. McCoy sees a giant talking white rabbit, straight out of *Alice in Wonderland,* being chased by a little girl, looking suspiciously like Alice, as illustrated in the book. Sulu is attacked by a Samurai warrior. And shortly thereafter McCoy is actually killed by a knight on horseback. Even Captain Kirk meets an old adversary from his school days and has a delicious fight with him. People and situations appear *just as one is thinking about them.* An old man shows up, who identifies himself as the caretaker of the planet and explains that the planet is an amusement park designed to instantly give guests what they imagine. Visitors can create either their amusements or dire circumstances. One cannot get more graphic in how the mind creates reality.

In the movie *The Secret* it is pointed out that sometimes it is not a good thing to have our thoughts translated instantly into reality, since it could lead to awkward or even dangerous circumstances. I believe it is possible to have instant manifestation of thought—such as when Jesus instantly healed the sick—but we have not evolved to a point where we can deal with that kind of power. Indeed, some people have not evolved to a point where they even believe they create their own reality. The most powerful tool for the manifestation of thought seems to be our words. What we *say* holds enormous power. In fact, the reason for chanting is based on the power of sound, and the "ohm" chant or the sound "ah" is said to be the sound we use for "God" universally. By chanting these before or during meditation it is believed we connect more authentically with our Source, which is God. The Bible speaks about the immense power of words. "Death and life are in the power of the tongue." (Proverbs 18:21) And the great modern-day metaphysician, Florence Scovel Shinn, whose book *Your Word Is Your Wand* influenced so many people around the world, said that man has the power to change an unhappy condition—*by waving over it the wand of his word.* As a friend's old grandmother used to say, "Watch what you wish for, because you might just get it."

Our Ultimate Potential

124

Errand of Mercy, the episode with which this book started, has a wealth of symbolism which could be the condensing of the whole premise of mankind's true nature and his evolution. From the Klingons, with their tribal, aggressive, and insular attitudes, through the *Enterprise* crew who are more altruistic, and on to the

Organians, whom we meet in this episode, we see at least three levels of potential existence.

The planet Organia is an important one for the Klingons to conquer in their ongoing battle with the United Federation of Planets. On an errand of mercy, Kirk and Spock disguise themselves as traders to try to stop this war. To their bewilderment, the Organian Council, consisting of four elderly men, are not only unconcerned about a war, they do not particularly appreciate Kirk and Spock's efforts.

What the officers don't know yet is that the Organians have long evolved from their need of a body and its limitations. Being around humans is distasteful to them because it reminds them of their origins. Not only have they evolved from bodily needs, and now exist as pure energy, but they can create reality instantly using mind power. They constructed buildings and other scenery and took human form because it is what the visitors would expect. They want their guests to be comfortable with their presence. In a final demonstration of *why* they are unconcerned about war, they neutralize the weapons on both sides by making them too hot to hold when the Klingons, Kirk, and Spock try to use them. In a moment of introspection, Kirk sees that he is not as evolved as he thought when he realizes he was relishing the prospect of a good fight.

Here is an example of absolute power. The Organians have evolved to a point where they can control anything and are at peace, but instead of using it to control other people they have chosen to be peacekeepers.

Becoming Pure Energy

In James Redfield's book, *The Celestine Prophecy,* he explains our ultimate evolutionary path akin to the episode, *Errand of Mercy.* He says, "Our destiny is to increase our energy level. And as our energy level increases, the level of vibration in the atoms of our bodies increases." As we get "lighter," we get more purely spiritual. As our atoms increase in vibration, we eventually would be invisible to those of a lower vibration. (A demonstration of this was seen in the *Star Trek* episode *Wink of an Eye,* although the method of doing it was not exactly "spiritual.")

125

He further shows how this was demonstrated by Christ. "He opened up to the energy until He was so light he could walk on water. He transcended death right here on Earth, and was the first to cross over, to expand the physical world into the spiritual." He told us that all he could do, we could also, and even more. The way to do it was in his example of how to live our lives. Eventually, we would be able to just walk from this earth plane into our true form—pure energy. This is undoubtedly what some fundamentalist Christians refer to as the "Rapture," a word that is not in the Bible. However, it may not be something that happens outside of us because we are "chosen." It is an inside job. We are each responsible for our own rapture, although it is through connection with God, our Source, that it happens. God is within us, and when we truly connect with that Source energy, we rise in vibration as a result.

Redfield is not the only author who has been teaching this concept for many years; Wayne Dyer and Deepak Chopra are two of the more well-known personalities who have been explaining reality-illusion scenarios through their tapes, books, and personal appearances for at least 20 years. Their work is down to earth and easily understood by anyone who wants to access it. The principles are the same as *A Course in Miracles*—nothing is real except by your own perception. If you don't like what you have decided your life is, then decide something else. You have written the script, chosen the characters, and produced the play. You can make any changes you wish.

The Original Star Trek Episodes

The original series of *Star Trek* seems somewhat different from the sequels. *Next Generation, Voyager, Deep Space Nine,* and *Enterprise* are more in line with adventure-crisis themes, with nothing really new regarding ideas such as these. In the original series, the concepts were unique, but by the time we were introduced to the subsequent ones, we were accustomed to the metaphysical vision of the first 79 presentations. It was about 20 years before the second series, *Star Trek the Next Generation,* appeared on our screens. Many times the later plots just re-wrote versions of earlier ones. To be sure, moral standards were observed in subsequent series, but there was something almost prophetic about the original episodes' dramatization of the dawning of insight about how the mind works, how it creates reality, and about our own evolution as a species.

126

Is it possible that we are guided by a higher intelligence that still sends prophets or guides to condition us on several levels simultaneously to accept and integrate new concepts as we evolve spiritually? I believe Gene Roddenberry and his group were one such guiding force whether they realized it or not. Helen Schucman, the scribe behind *A Course in Miracles*, was another such avatar, as were her friends, Bill Thetford and Kenneth Wapnick.

A loving father will reach his children best by teaching them on a level where they are. He would not talk above them or below them or in a language they do not understand. And we know, as parents, that a loving father is concerned about *all* his children, not just the ones who behave well. I believe that when we are on the verge of a breakthrough in consciousness, a prophet, avatar, or leader appears to address a group with whom he relates. Each could be teaching and explaining new concepts simultaneously in many different media venues according to his group's most comfortable and familiar mode of expression. Those who enjoy TV dramas can be reached by something like *Star Trek*. Moviegoers have *The Matrix* as just one example. There are other movies having this theme of reality versus illusion—especially in the last few years. Religious groups will find their avatars in their midst addressing them in their own comfort zone, and many readers will relate to something like *A Course in Miracles*, which is a book—or rather, three books in one. Scientific types need to know the physics behind it, so quantum mechanics became more widely accepted and understood around the mid-20th century.

There were probably many other unknown creative teachers in the Sixties and Seventies who had this same message—**you create your own reality by what you give passion and attention to, and our world is an illusion of our own making**—but I think we can safely say that the message is "taking" today. We are truly on the verge of a giant shift in our collective agreement about what is real and what is not. *Star Trek* contributed very significantly to this shift, perhaps the greatest shift so far in our history as a planet, and the series wouldn't have survived so long were it not perhaps our best allegory of this shift. Hopefully, we will live up to its wisdom and astonishing vision.

Note:

The two remaining chapters consider the astrology of *Star Trek* and look at the birth charts of Gene Roddenberry and Helen Schucman. The chapters are written to be understood by people with little background in astrology, so if you are interested in this aspect, read on!

Following these two chapters is a brief list of books and websites related to the spiritual themes we touched on in this book.

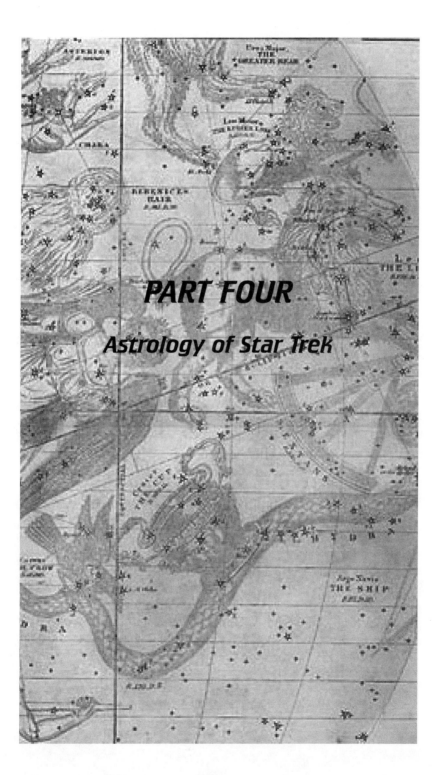

PART FOUR

Astrology of Star Trek

CHAPTER THIRTEEN

Our Cosmic Clock—it was _time_ for Star Trek!

> *What was born during the 1960s (in an admittedly wrenching caesarian section) was not merely a discontinuity in American and world history, but a harbinger of things to come. That Uranus-Pluto awakening—in all its joy and disturbance, its spiritual searching, alternate lifestyles, social disobedience, and even its violent confrontations—represented the birth pangs of conflicts that will return in the years ahead, but in manifestations and for reasons very different from those of its boisterous infancy.*
>
> ~ Bill Herbst (www.billherbst.com)

Our planetary system is a big clock in the sky. I believe it is one of God's greatest gifts to us, showing us the unfolding of our earthly journey and establishing "time" for a variety of purposes—as it says in Genesis 1:14 and Ecclesiastes 3:1-8. In Genesis we are told the Sun and Moon would mark time and be used for "signs." The Magi, who were astrologers ("Magi" is from the root word that _means_ astrologer), saw the sign of the Messiah in this great clock and undertook a long and arduous journey of many months based on just this information. They saw his "star" (really a conjunction of Saturn and Jupiter) and came to worship. If God really considers astrology as being from the devil and therefore evil, then I doubt He would have sent an angel to lead them safely out of the Holy Land by a different route to avoid King Herod.

130

In Ecclesiastes 3 we are told: *"To every thing there is a season, and a time to every purpose under the heaven: A time to be born, and a time to die....."* How do we know what time it is for what? By learning to tell time by the great clock in the sky, our solar system.

The Sun is a star, and without it we would not survive—at least not in our earthly bodies. When we speak of "astro" (star) in the word astrology, we are not necessarily limiting it to the constellations. It includes our own *Sun* and its influence on us, which is undeniable. And now with the revelations we are having regarding the behavior of subatomic particles, we are discovering that something as far away and small as Pluto—as well as the constellations—*can indeed* influence us.

Astrology is a study of cycles, and one of the most reliable cycles that times major changes and "rebirthing" processes in humanity's journey is the Uranus-Pluto cycle. The cycle begins at the conjunction of the two (when they appear to be "aligned" in space), which occurs once every 140-145 years. The last conjunction, or "birth" of a new cycle, was from 1963 to 1969. Since Uranus is faster than Pluto, it pulls away from the alignment, and about a quarter of the way through the cycle will be 90 degrees from Pluto. That will be an important point in their cyclical dance when we will see manifestations relevant to the events that occurred at the conjunction. Halfway through the cycle, Uranus will be opposite Pluto, another important reminder of what we birthed back at the beginning of the cycle, and then the last 90-degree point will be reached three-quarters of the way along their journey, and then back to another conjunction and the opportunity for a new global enlightening growth experience. From roughly late 2011 through early 2018 we will be reaching the first quarter phase of the current cycle. We can expect to be reminded of what we experienced when the cycle began in the mid-Sixties. That means we will have an opportunity to build on what was started then.

The Sixties was a turbulent decade. We experienced dramas that were unique when compared to those that went before and followed after. The main theme was rebellion and expression of individual opinion and power. This was also the theme of the previous alignment during the middle of the 1820s. This is understandable given the *meanings* of the two planets involved, Uranus and Pluto.

Archetypal Meanings 131

Each planet has archetypal meanings that apply as much today as they did centuries ago. They apply on an individual level as well as on the collective. We are subliminally conditioned to this by our very language. We say someone has a "jovial" disposition, which is a reference to Jupiter. Another is said to be "martial" in temperament, meaning "warlike," and "martial arts" is a reference to the art of combat. This is an accurate portrayal of the meaning of Mars in our lives. The expression "venereal disease" comes from a reference to Venus, the planet that represents social interaction. When we hear the word Venus we immediately think of beauty and love. This is not an accident. It has been a part of our collective culture and psyche for centuries and comes from astrology.

Not so commonly known are the archetypal meanings of Uranus and Pluto. Uranus is the archetype of independence and individuality. People who have this planet strongly placed in their birth charts (which depends, in part, on the time of day one is born) resist being controlled by others and strive to be free at all costs as they go through their lives. They are the rebels, the pioneers, and the agents of social change. Usually, they are self-employed or unhappy being under someone else's jurisdiction.

Pluto represents power and control. If change happens at all, it would be explosive and total. Plutonium is well named. We also relate to the words "plutocrat" and "plutocracy" as all-controlling. Pluto is the archetype of hidden or subversive control. We are reminded of the Mafia. People with Pluto strong in their birth charts are usually not what they seem and have an almost pathological need to control and can be most vengeful. However, everything has a positive and negative polarity. The positive side of this archetype is the destroying of an old order so that the fresh air of change and rebirth can emerge—like the burning off of old crops to refresh the field for new seedlings to flourish.

On a deeper level, Pluto represents the unconscious mind in a person and humanity's collective unconscious. In a personal chart, an astrologer can see how much an individual comes from an unconscious level and conversely, how aware that person is of motivations for behavior. On a collective level, when we see these cycles involving Pluto, we can tell when the collective masses will have their attention drawn to their own subversive or enlightened behavior, whichever the case may be.

132

Uranus Meets Pluto

When I am doing a client's personal chart, and I see that the current position of Uranus in space is coming to the person's birth position of Pluto (or vice versa), I can confidently say the person will rebel against the status quo (if there is anything the client is not happy with), and that it will be *total.* Most of the time, it is over-done. I call it the "throwing out the baby with the bathwater" syndrome. Usually, it is explosive, sudden, and often irreversible. It doesn't happen often, given the lengthy orbits of these planets, but it is always a life-changing time. Uranus is called "the great awakener," and when it contacts Pluto in a person's birth chart, the client "awakens" (Uranus) to whatever "control" (Pluto) there may be that has become unbearable and strives to change it totally.

It can also be the discovery of subversion, itself—like finding out about something that was secret. Uranus, as an energy, urges us to take risks, to express independence, and so we behave a little more rashly, and possibly out of character, in order to free ourselves of perceived controlling mechanisms. Some people in general, and at different times, are more affected than others. We refer to a planet's placement in space by its sign and degree position. Right now Uranus is traversing Pisces and those people born in late February to late March of any year have been experiencing this kind of urge to freedom. It will go on until early 2011, affecting each Pisces in order of their birth date, with those born very late in the sign experiencing this energy in 2009 through 2011; those born early in the sign have already had the experience since 2003.

Uranus stays in any given sign for an average of seven years. Pluto is not so even in its orbit, and when it comes inside the orbit of Neptune in its elliptical path around the Sun, it goes through signs faster than when it is farther away, outside the orbit of Neptune. At the longest it can take 30 years to traverse a sign, and at the shortest less than a dozen years. Therefore, this cycle's timing can vary greatly depending on where Pluto is in its irregular journey around the Sun.

When these two come into alignment (and at the 90 and 180 degree points in their cycle) in their orbits in the heavens, we all globally awaken to whatever conditions we find unbearable. We rebel, and it is explosive, sometimes violent, and often irreversible. Think about the Sixties. It was unprecedented in our expression of rebellion from Woodstock to Vietnam War protests to a sexual revolution to multiple assassinations. The people *born* during this time carry the pattern that was being expressed, and when they reach control in governments throughout the world, that seed of rebellion will bear fruit. It will be around the time of the first 90-degree point of this great cycle—2011 through 2018.

133

People Born in the Sixties

The birth chart is not just a forecasting device. It is also a portrait of the owner. All of the people born from 1963 to 1969 have some traits in common. They all have Pluto conjunct Uranus in Virgo in their birth chart—some more strongly placed than others, of course. As a sub-generation, this is quite significant. I had three children before 1963 and one after 1969, so I was a young parent at the time and was friends with many women who had jobs like nursing and teaching. The teachers particularly— and independently, I might add—came to me with the same question. "What IS it with these kids going into first grade this year?" This was around 1969 when the 1963 babies were entering elementary school. Also, I had friends who were the mothers of some of these children, and they, too, noticed a distinct difference in the children born in these years. For one thing, they were "teenagers" at two. Their willfulness was extreme. They were very "picky" about things, from what they wore to what they ate. They also had a very discriminating way of getting to the core of an issue and cutting through the chaff.

It was also during the Sixties that we went back to nature and began being concerned about the preservatives and chemicals we were putting into our bodies. Food co-ops were formed, and many hardy souls began to grow their own food who had never done so before. Whoever is born at a particular time carries the qualities of that time with them for life, to paraphrase the Swiss psychologist Carl Jung, who used astrology extensively in his work. And so, like those in the Sixties who were careful about what they ate and were rebellious with the status quo, people *born* at that time are also going to exhibit the same values and traits.

What Does This Have to Do with Star Trek?

Star Trek and *A Course in Miracles* were both "born" in the Sixties. They have a similar message, and I believe a similar purpose. Both were awakeners to breaking up old concepts we held on an unconscious level and to bring new ideas that perhaps life works a little differently than we thought it did. Each in its own way taught us that life is an illusion of our own making. The core teaching of *A Course in Miracles* is:

"*Nothing real can be threatened.*
Nothing unreal exists.
Herein lies the peace of God."

134

Star Trek taught similar themes from time to time, but in a way that was entertaining and painless. However, when the subconscious recognizes a truth, it resonates with it. That is why *Star Trek* has endured for nearly half a century. It was *time* for its message, and we were ready for it. When these large cycles of the outer planets reach points of transition, humanity responds. Another way of looking at the key meanings of Uranus and Pluto is an "awakening" (Uranus) *of* the "collective unconscious" (Pluto). In other words, it was time in our collective evolution to wake up to new ways of understanding what "reality" is and what the "unconscious" is, how the unconscious operates in our lives and how we can better use it to our benefit—for example, to create the kind of reality we would prefer. This is what happens each time these two planets begin a new cycle. Each time we grow a bit more and our vibrations rise as we evolve into what is possible for us to spiritually become.

CHAPTER FOURTEEN

Significant Charts

> *Since you want to know my opinion about astrology I can tell you that I've been interested in this particular activity of the human mind since more than 30 years. As I am a psychologist, I am chiefly interested in the particular light the horoscope sheds on certain complications in the character. In cases of difficult psychological diagnosis I usually get a horoscope in order to have a further point of view from an entirely different angle. I must say that I very often found that the astrological data elucidated certain points, which I otherwise would have been unable to understand. From such experiences I formed the opinion that astrology is of particular interest to the psychologist, since it contains a sort of psychological experience which we call "projected"—this means that we find the psychological facts as it were in the constellations.*
>
> ~ Carl Gustav Jung

As far as the timing of appearance of these two works (*Star Trek* and *A Course in Miracles*) is concerned, we have to examine the charts of Gene Roddenberry and Helen Schucman, their creators, to see how they were affected by the Uranus/Pluto alignment at the time. We also have to examine the charts of the first airing of *Star Trek* compared to Mr. Roddenberry's, as well as the first scribing of *A Course in Miracles* compared to Helen Schucman's natal chart. I will try to make this as clear and understandable as I can for readers unfamiliar with astrology.

An accurately timed astrological chart is like an X-ray of the character. It shows what a person has been born with in terms of his innate attributes. Anyone can determine this with just a little study of the basic astrological tenets, which are *not* horoscope columns in the newspaper—a prostitution of this extraordinary science. Besides being an X-ray of the character, the birth chart is also a timing device showing the timing of events in that person's life. It is as reliable as the Sun rising and setting, since it is based on the same celestial rhythms. Also, everyone is pure potential when they are born, but certain traits or character habits are in place when we take our first breath. What we do with them later is completely in our hands.

When turning points in these great cycles—or even minor cycles—affect a specific person's chart, he can be more affected by them than others. The response can be more personal than a cycle change that affects everyone. For example, the Uranus-Pluto conjunction affected the whole planet, but it affected individuals quite differently depending on the strength and placement of Uranus and Pluto in their birth charts. Both Roddenberry and Schucman were clearly born to ride the energies of this great wave.

First, what kind of man did Gene Roddenberry's chart show he was when we look at the "X-ray"?

Gene Roddenberry's Character

Mr. Roddenberry was born compassionate, innovative, and fearless in his ability to push beyond the status quo. Several features in his chart show vivid imagination and even some psychic ability. His creativity, as we would assume, was also extremely high. He would stick to projects and see them to conclusion, since he had an almost obsessive quality about personal projects or anything he loved. He also saw things in a large, all-encompassing way— the big picture. He was a homebody, but could have been a little controlling. He would have chalked it up to being concerned about his loved ones—and he did care deeply about those he loved. He was also a perfectionist, particularly about his home and his work. He did not like things too much out of place and would have probably known where all his possessions were left when he last used them.

Above all, there is a cluster of planets in Leo. Leo needs to feel he has left a legacy of some sort. All Leos like recognition, but the underlying psychological need is to feel he has left something of himself behind to live beyond him, whether it is a biological child or a "brainchild" of creative work. Mr. Roddenberry had a

137

restlessness to be doing something creative all the time. He must have had a whole raft of ideas flowing constantly. The planets involved in the cluster are Mars, Neptune, Mercury, and the Sun. This combination is imaginative, creative, mentally active in the extreme, but also sensitive and kind. To add to his sensitivity, he had Cancer rising and the Moon in Pisces—both indicative of sensitivity, kindness, and understanding.

Amazingly, the two planets that defined the Sixties, Uranus and Pluto, are *strong* in Mr. Roddenberry's *birth* chart. Pluto is rising. That means that Pluto was coming up over the eastern horizon around the *minute* he was born. That position is called the ascendant, and it changes an average of one degree (of a circle, representing the earth's rotation) every four minutes of clock time. That is the strongest position in any chart, and if a planet is present there at the time of birth, it gains enormous influence in that person's life. If he had been born a half hour later, that strength would have been gone. People with Pluto rising are strong, persistent souls who can easily be innovators bringing complete change to whatever they touch. He did things on *Star Trek* that no one had ever done before. For instance, he insisted on a multi-cultural crew and gave a black woman a very prominent respectful role to play. This was unheard of at the time. *Star Trek* also dared to air the first interracial kiss—another taboo—in the episode *Plato's Stepchildren*.

Uranus in his chart is conjunct the Moon. In other words, at the minute he was born, the Moon was in alignment with Uranus in space. This gives strength to Uranus in his chart. Anyone with this alignment is unusual—often possessing genius of some kind—but also unpredictable, easily bored, restless, and highly innovative. In Pisces, this conjunction would indicate being highly sensitive to the need for everyone to be free to pursue their dreams. He would see "freedom" as an emotional security need for all people. I would imagine it was this alignment that was behind the concept of *Star Trek*'s future culture's freedom from having to attend to economic survival needs so that each person could develop his capabilities to the fullest.

138

Fast Forward to 1966

I am showing a simplified chart to illustrate what was going on with Mr. Roddenberry's chart at the time of the first airing of *Star Trek*. The inner wheel is his birth chart, and the outer wheel is where the planets were at the time the show started—

when it was "born." I have labeled the "angles" of the chart. MC stands for Medium Coeli or "midheaven." IC stands for Imum Coeli, which is the fourth house cusp and the midnight position of the chart. Some people call it the Nadir, but that is a misnomer. (For astrology buffs, the nadir is the opposite of the zenith, which is the pole of the horizon. These are points directly overhead and directly below. The MC or IC may or may not coincide with these points. Many people incorrectly use the terms interchangeably.) The AC stands for the Ascendant and DC stands for the Descendant. These four angles are totally dependent on the *time* anyone or anything is born. They change rapidly and make one whole revolution each day, since they are based on the Earth's rotation. In a person's chart, they are called the "personal points." Twins might have them a degree apart or more, and it is the main indicator of their differences, at least chart-wise.

Significant changes in people's lives are usually indicated by activity around these angles, whether it is a contact coming from a mathematical system or a "transit" from the current planetary positions in real time. The kind of change, I've come to learn, depends on the mindset or attitude of the person owning the chart. Anything can be positive and vice versa. But the timing of the change will be predictable.

When the activity is connected to the MC and/or IC, it will involve the person's life on a core foundational level and usually is connected with career. When it is with the AC or DC, it will involve relationships. You can see in Figure 1, that when the series first aired, Pluto and Uranus, which were conjunct in Virgo most of the decade, were straddling Mr. Roddenberry's IC. His very foundation was shaken from this event, and it was positive for him. For some other person without his optimism and positive attitude, it could have been a very negative event. There were many other indications of major change in his life, but we are only discussing the Pluto/Uranus alignment of the Sixties at this time. Obviously it affected Mr. Roddenberry on a very personal level, ushering in a major shift in his life.

Gene Roddenberry

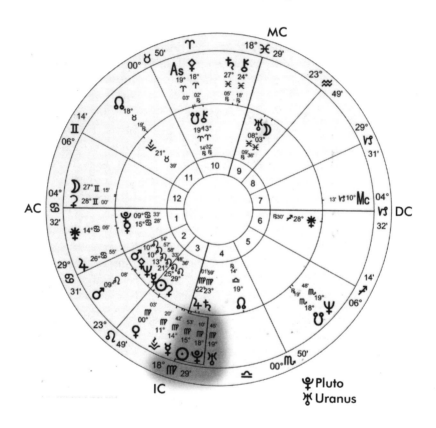

Figure 1

Helen Schucman

Born on July 14, 1909, Helen Schucman was a spiritual seeker her whole life and a clinical psychologist in New York City. She took dictation from the voice of Jesus for several years, culminating in the three-volume set of books (now published as one volume), *A Course in Miracles.* It began when Jesus said the words, "This is a course in miracles; please take notes." Many Christian teachings are clarified, but above all the theme is forgiveness, that unconditional love of our brothers as we love ourselves is required before we can return to oneness with the Father, and that we *are* all one. Additionally, the theme that we are in an illusion of our *own* making, not God's, is explained and made clear.

The actual scribing began on October 21, 1965, and the books were first published in June, 1976. Using dates of significant events in her life, it appears that she could have been born around 6:00 a.m. Even without a time of birth, her chart shows the timing of the scribing quite well. As an aside, she and Roddenberry both were born with Neptune conjoining personal planets, which indicates sensitivity to psychic phenomenon. There are many other similarities. At the time of her scribing the Course, the conjunction of Pluto and Uranus was 90 degrees from her nodal axis and also her Moon. The nodes are points on the Ecliptic where the Moon would cross it, IF it were crossing at any given time. When it *does* actually cross the Ecliptic, it is an eclipse. The Moon's nodes are very important, for it is here that we can interpret why a person has been born and what the karmic path is in general terms. Her task in this life was to think for herself and find her own answers, which she obviously did admirably. She was also to learn to be ego-less, having had past lives of admiration and personal attention. She has remained relatively unknown despite her phenomenal contribution. In fact, many people think Marianne Williamson wrote *A Course in Miracles,* since she is a well-known advocate of the work.

We are taught that we have guides on the other side who will help us when we ask, but they cannot do anything unless we request it. Helen had a personality that did not like discord. At Columbia University, where she worked, she and colleague, Bill Thetford, had a difficult relationship, not only with each other but with other professional colleagues there. In frustration, Bill said one day in June 1965, "There must be a better way." They resolved to change the way they were reacting to all provocation.

This was apparently the request needed to get guidance. When Helen took Jesus' dictation, she would give the result to Bill the following morning to type. He was very involved in the production of the Course, which was giving them the "better way" they wanted.

There were other significant indications in her chart that she had a "job" to do, and the time had come to do it. It would be too complex to explain here. A good biography of Helen Schucman is *Absence from Felicity* by Kenneth Wapnick, PhD, her close friend in later years.

Helen Schucman

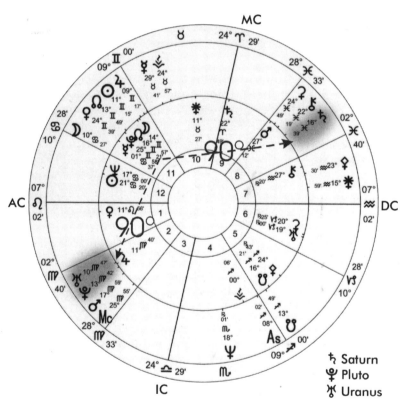

Figure 2

Note: Transits are for June 1965 when she and Bill Thetford first asked for "a better way."

Star Trek's Birth Chart

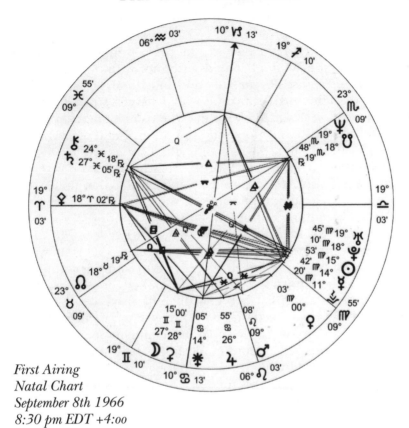

First Airing
Natal Chart
September 8th 1966
8:30 pm EDT +4:oo

Anything that is comes into existence has a birth chart. The chart describes the personality of the entity being born, whether it is a person, a city, a cocktail party or a play. Anything and everything that debuts has a chart. For a dramatic presentation, it is the moment the drama first begins in public. The writing, rehearsals and other preparation comprise the gestation period or "pregnancy." Star Trek was born on September 8, 1966 at 8:30 pm EST according to The Star Trek Compendium by Allan Asherman. However, daylight savings time was in effect then, so more than likely it was 8:30 EDT since TV listings are printed in the time in effect. It makes a huge difference.

The rising sign in any chart is the most personal point and describes the personality or projected image of the subject. It is a fast-moving point based on the Earth's rotation and all twelve

143

signs rise within the span of one day. It is based on the time of birth from a specific longitude and latitude. Even in the case of a drama that is scheduled at a particular time, the "personality" of the project will still project as the chart indicates.

In the standard time chart, Taurus is rising. That would not describe the action oriented series nor its innovative spirit. Taurus is sensuous, slow-moving and sometimes stubborn. It is artistic, though, and I think we would have seen much more opulence in the sets had it been the true rising sign. Aries rising, however, would show action and innovation, and that is what we have with the daylight savings time chart. Aries symbolizes the pioneer, the warrior, the explorer which more suits the series' main theme. Also, Aries is impulsive and exists in the "now"—the way the whole series was produced.

At the beginning of the series, the NBC heads did not really like the series or have a great deal of hope for it. The MC is the point that represents authority, and in this chart that is shown by Saturn (because Capricorn is on the MC and Saturn is connected with that sign). Saturn is 90 degrees from the Moon. This means that there was a conflict between the authority over the series and the ones who worked with it every day. It is also the source of the bad reviews it got. The Moon is in Gemini in the third house, both of which represent communications about the series. One of the reasons it ultimately was so popular is shown by Saturn being 120 degrees (a trine) from Jupiter. Jupiter is representative of the grass roots populace, since it is in the fourth sector. That means it was loved by the masses and touched a chord in their psyche. It also is connected to the ninth house, which is mass opinion and broadcasting. The trine between Saturn and Jupiter is very strong, being only 10 minutes from exactness, but there is the exact same strength between the Saturn and Moon 90 degree aspect (called a square). Based on just this, the show could have gone either way. It was all over in three years coinciding with the Moon changing signs by solar arc. Even if it had not ended, it would have changed in some basic way.

The infamous Uranus/Pluto alignment is in the sixth house conjoining the Sun and Mercury. That is very powerful and describes the daily panic and pressure the show was under. Innovation is the province of Uranus. With their all being in Virgo, there was purity about the show that was like a service being performed for humanity. The sixth sector is about service through work and producing something of value. All of these

144

bodies are in sextile aspect (60 degrees) to Neptune which represents creative imagination and spirituality. Neptune is located in Scorpio, noted for passion and transformation. A sextile aspect is opportunity with no guarantee of success. Putting it together, this is a service with an opportunity to transform spiritually through creative imagination.

Every sign is ruled by a planet, and the ruler of the ascending sign is very important. In this case, Aries is always ruled by Mars, and Mars here is in the fifth house which is drama. It is also about children, who were the first targeted audience. Mars is in Leo which is also drama. Any astrologer looking at this chart and not knowing whose or what event's it is, would conclude that this entity is a dramatic pioneer, impulsive but also with the soul of service.

Success

The bottom line, though, is that the show was a phenomenal long term success. What shows that in the chart? The soul of a chart is the Sun. It influences our very lives. Therefore, the place to look for success is to the Sun and how it is configured with the rest of the chart—particularly the MC. In this case the Sun, Mercury, Uranus and Pluto—all of them—are in trine aspect to the MC. That is, they are all within range of being 120 degrees from that point. I don't know for a fact, but I'd be willing to venture that it was understood how successful it was about 9 ½ years after the show first aired. It didn't begin to be realized at all until about 4 ½ years afterward. The chart shows it took that long for its success to be realized. The promise of it, however, was always there.

We Are On Time

We are told in the Bible that "every hair on your head is counted" and that there is "a time to every purpose under heaven." We need not worry that we will miss something or that we are going to be abandoned. The Course says that if we knew who walked beside us on this journey through life, fear would be impossible. We need only love unconditionally and not be guilty of judgment. It brings indescribable peace.

145

RESOURCES

Here are some of the books, films, and websites for exploring the spiritual themes we've touched on in this book:

A Course in Miracles. Originally three separate volumes (Text, Workbook for Students, and the Manual for Teachers), the set is now published as a single volume. Its purpose is to help us "remove the blocks to the awareness of love's presence" by teaching the true nature of guilt and forgiveness and how our subconscious guilt can be cleared by forgiving the traits we dislike or judge in others. Once these qualities are forgiven in others, they are automatically cleared for us as well. And it is guilt that is the main blockage to our awareness of love's presence in us. One of the concepts especially relevant to this book is that miracles actually collapse time, a shortening that is smoothed out or adjusted by the Holy Spirit. The website is www.fipdata.org/index.html.

Abraham teachings. These are presented through Esther Hicks and represent perhaps the best elucidation we have of what is called the Law of Attraction. The meaning of this law, stated simply, is that your experience of reality is completely determined by what you pay attention to. If you focus on what you don't want all the time, through complaining and noticing what's wrong in various departments of your life, then you effectively create a set of future experiences that will perfectly match this focus. If on the other hand, you learn to amplify your focus on what you would consider ideal (or even just a *little* better than what you have now), then this focus will soon begin to manifest as your experience. The beauty of the Abraham material is that it shows us through hundreds of audience questions exactly how to do all of this and inspires us to keep at it until we have become "deliberate creators" of our own experience.   147

Key Abraham books include *The Law of Attraction: The Basics of the Teachings of Abraham* and *Ask and It Is Given.* The website is www.abraham-hicks.com.

Esther/Abraham also appear on the DVD, *The Secret,* a beautifully produced presentation about the key truths and applications of the Law of Attraction, from many perspectives. Available from bookstores or www.thesecret.tv/home.html.

Astrology. There are many good books and courses out there, including the classic *Astrology: A Cosmic Science,* by Isabel Hickey. Carole Devine's own website is www.devineadvantage.com.

Conversations with God, by Neale Donald Walsch. A series of books centering on the idea that God is not a Person "out there," but one with everything and one with each of us. The books record conversations that are inspired, rather than channeled. One of the great founts of wisdom.

Edgar Cayce, the most documented psychic of the twentieth century. His 14,000 "readings" are available on a single searchable CD and cover every conceivable subject, from Atlantis to reincarnation and holistic healing. Cayce's Association for Research and Enlightenment (the A.R.E.) is located in Virginia Beach, VA. The website is www.edgarcayce.org.

Gary Zukav, author of *The Dancing Wu Li Masters,* wrote the first great book on the new physics. Your worldview will never be the same. His *Seat of the Soul* is a masterpiece.

Deepak Chopra, author of many books in both philosophy and healing. They are *all* worth reading.

148

Love Without End: Jesus Speaks, by Glenda Green. An astonishing book, which begins with a portrait artist hearing that she will be painting the portrait of Jesus Christ. He appears one day in her studio and during the course of the painting, Jesus explains to Glenda how the heart has its own intelligence, far exceeding the intelligence of the mind. He covers virtually every topic of importance to humankind.

Jane Roberts, the Seth books: *Seth Speaks* and *The Nature of Personal Reality,* among many others. The two over arching concepts are probably our personal responsibility for our own experience and the parallel-lives idea, both of which appear often as themes in *Star Trek.* www.seth-speaks.com. One of the more fascinating books in the series is *The Education of Oversoul Seven,* which shows how our oversouls develop by observing and carefully helping their earth lives (souls) being lived in parallel (even though the lives would appear to us as sequential).

James Redfield, author of *The Celestine Prophecy* and two sequels (a third is in the works), covers many topics, but one key principle is that the more elevated the consciousness, the more synchronicity is experienced. This principle dovetails perfectly with "entanglement," parallel lives, the Field, and the One Spirit, all of which are saying that time is not the linear dimension we thought it was, that simultaneity rules, for those who are sensitive to it.

Masaru Emoto's book, *The Hidden Messages in Water,* is one of the great "paradigm-busters" of our age. The very idea that *anything* could affect the way water crystallizes as it freezes would have been regarded by most people as merely someone's fantasy, until Emoto's experimental research established the effect. More astonishing still is the observation that even the vibrations of written words taped to the glass have a discernible effect: Written prayers produce beautiful crystals, whereas written curses produce very deformed crystals. Also see his DVD, which shows the crystallizations as they appear. His website is www.masaru-emoto.net/english/entop.html.

Mike Dooley. Mike appears on the DVD, *The Secret,* and is one of the acknowledged master teachers of the Law of Attraction. His website is www.tut.com.

149

Richard Bach, author of *One,* as well as many other profoundly eye-opening books, gives us perhaps the best illustration of the idea that different choices lead to parallel experiences.

Robert Monroe is the great pioneer of scientific research into out-of-body experiences. His book, *Journeys Out of the Body,* is the classic in its field, and he later founded the Monroe Institute near Charlottesville, VA, as a research and workshop center.

Using Monroe's hemi-sync technology to help you access higher levels of consciousness, the Center allows you to visit places and to meet beings whose existence you would never have even suspected. The website is www.monroeinstitute.com.

Like most of the other authors in this list, Monroe did not consider time to be linear. He reported once that he had gone back in time and comforted a young Roman soldier who had just died in battle, and the positive effect introduced an audible alteration into the entire timeline between then and Monroe's current life. The young soldier turned out to be one of Monroe's earlier incarnations.

The Field, by Lynne McTaggart, one of the truly ground breaking books of recent years, describes the scientific research leading to the idea of the one, indivisible field that underlies and interpenetrates everything that exists. It is very easy to read, and you will come away from it a changed person.

By explaining entanglement and related phenomena, McTaggart shows how contemporary science has established that since the speed of light *cannot* be the limit of communication, there must be some kind of unified field that instantaneously conveys information between twin particles that have been separated by such a distance that even the speed of light is too slow for the information to be conveyed between them. Compare this with *Love Without End,* which has a great deal of easy-to-follow scientific information and which says that the unified field of which McTaggart speaks is the physical manifestation of the One Spirit.

150

Wayne Dyer, author of numerous books, such as *Inspiration: Your Ultimate Calling* and *The Power of Intention: Learning to Co-create Your World Your Way* is one of the foremost speakers and writers of our time. Many of his topics relate to the philosophy of *Star Trek.*

What the Bleep Do We Know!? A movie and DVD, followed by *What the Bleep Do We Know!?– Down the Rabbit Hole.* These two films have gone far in uniting science and spirituality, something close to the heart of Gene Roddenberry.